Before You Buy
You Buy
Word
Processing
Software

Dona Z. Meilach

CROWN PUBLISHERS, INC., NEW YORK

1287-29

To Mel Meilach
and Allen Meilach

Published by Crown Publishers, Inc., One Park
Avenue, New York, New York 10016, and
simultaneously in Canada by General Publishing
Company Limited
Manufactured in the United States of America
Library of Congress Cataloging in Publication
Data
Meilach, Dona Z.
    Before you buy word processing software.
    Includes index.
    1. Word processing—Computer programs—
Purchasing.
I. Title.
Z52.4.M44   1984   652   84-4305
ISBN 0-517-44339-2 (cloth)
ISBN 0-517-55340-6 (pbk.)
10   9   8   7   6   5   4   3   2   1
First Edition

Contents

Acknowledgments

I wish to thank the companies that provided software for evaluation. Specific programs can be found in the chapters where they apply.

For hardware, I am indebted to the AMDEK Corporation for an AMDEK Color-II Monitor, an MAI board, and floppy disk drives for use with the IBM PC, to the Kaypro Corporation for a Kaypro 4, and to the Zobex Corporation for continued support of my original Zobex computer.

I am grateful to the companies that provided photos; their names are credited beneath the product illustrated.

Special thanks to Allen Meilach, Ralph Ritchie, and Roy Paul for their cooperation, for double and triple checking technical details and my instructions in the text.

I am most appreciative to editor Les Spindle, assistant Sheila Ball, and publishers Robert and Nancy Jones of *Interface Age* magazine. Several chapters in the book are adapted and updated from articles I wrote which originally appeared in *Interface Age.*

In addition to marvelous help from everyone, my husband, Dr. Melvin Meilach, merits greatest gratitude. He could qualify for top membership with honors in a club for computer widowers. He has gallantly and stoically watched me, and watched over me, as I bent over the keyboard for hours, days, weeks, months, communicating with my terminal.

Dona Z. Meilach
Carlsbad, CA

NOTE: Every effort has been made to present all information correctly but because of the nature of the industry, its rapid changes, and constantly updated software, there is no guarantee or warranty implied by the author or the publisher regarding program procedures, prices, addresses, telephone numbers, and distributors.

Introduction

Before You Buy Word Processing Software introduces software and ideas that go beyond information contained in beginning books about word processing. It treats word processing as the key that opens the door to a treasure house of additional programs, areas for exploration, and procedures for combining them all creatively. You will learn what is available, be shown how it works, and see the result. The book encourages you to be a comparison shopper and provides the features on which to base your judgments.

Before You Buy Word Processing Software will be welcomed, I believe, by office managers who must make decisions for many people and by individuals searching for ways in which word processing can be more satisfying, effective, and efficient.

Each chapter discusses a specific type of program: word processing itself, spelling checkers, punctuation, thesaurus, document sectioning, the use of macros, training, utilities and working hints, and more. Programs normally not associated with word processing are presented when they can serve the discipline advantageously. Where applicable, charts are provided to show what each program offers, and what each lacks.

Every program explained has been implemented. Some have features that I don't like as well as another's. But other people have different preferences. I have avoided generalizations but I have not included any program I feel is worthless. Where one program is clumsy, or another is difficult to use and learn, this has been noted.

With so many programs on the market, so few available from local dealers, it is often impossible to know what a program can do before it is purchased. It takes time to study procedures and potential limitations of several similar programs, but it will help you weed out those that are wrong for your needs.

It's all here—the programs, the tools to expand word processing—with ideas for using the programs creatively so the computer can become the ultimate tool for your writing needs.

<u>Before</u> You Buy Word Processing Software

1. Wanting It All— and More!

he features of word processing are myriad and complex. If you're considering word processing for the first time, fathoming the meaning of many unfamiliar terms and what the commands can accomplish is not easy. The information presented in each chapter will increase your awareness of capabilities beyond basic word processing.

Veteran word processers, familiar with many procedures, raise new sets of questions and impose greater demands on the systems. Many who purchased word processing software before they knew the potential for the technology want to upgrade or change from their present system. Why? The program they bought does not have all the features they want, it won't integrate with other programs they would like to use, or it doesn't perform as elegantly as they would like. And, inevitably, new companies offer enhanced programs with hard-to-resist improvements.

First time users who want to know what to look for will benefit from questions asked by advanced users, such as:

☐ **What is the best word processor for my purposes?**

This means the user will have to state his purposes and find out what a program can and cannot do. Not too long ago the number of programs on the market for any one system could be counted on two hands. Today, there are an estimated 300 word processing programs and several choices for any one computer system.

☐ **There are many situations where my current word processing program won't accomplish what I want it to. Are additional manipulations possible? If so, how? With what?**

A word processing program is designed to enter text, edit it, format it, and send it to a printer. That's expected, like a chef in a fast food restaurant knowing how to fry hamburgers. But some top-notch chefs can whip up gourmet dinners effortlessly, present everything well, and add a few surprises. Then there are all the others in between. Word processing programs seem to be written by people with a similar range of capabilities.

If you are familiar with one word processing program, consult the list in Chapter 2, Your Personal Word Processing Program Profile (page 21), to learn the features that are available (no one program has all). Check the features in your current program with those now available. If another program promises more features that you want and greater flexibility and efficiency, will it be worth changing and learning a new set of commands? Perhaps your current program can position the cursor with only 8 moves, but another program may offer 14 methods for moving it about.

☐ **If I'm going to consider another program, it has to improve on what I have, but offer more. I don't know what "more" means. I don't know what else I can get. What can I expand to?**

These frequently posed questions, and others, with abundant discussion and examples, will be addressed in the following chapters. You'll discover what can be accomplished beyond the basic word processing, the programs that do it, how they work, how you may evaluate them, and where to find them. When there is a choice of programs, where applicable, a summary will be offered for several so you can compare one against another. When you assemble your own personal word processing wish list you'll know which features you need and how to recognize the programs that have them.

You will be introduced to spelling checkers, thesaurus programs, footnoting, endnoting, and bibliography generators. You'll discover how lengthy documents can be sectioned and, at the same time, how to create a table of contents (which can do double duty as a project outline). Anyone who must produce a project from beginning to final printed form will learn about features that can cross-reference documents and generate an index. If a page or chapter is added or deleted, the index is instantly corrected with the page references automatically replaced.

You'll be exposed to nonword processing programs that can increase word processing efficiency. Spreadsheet or "calc" programs can be used to create charts; merge programs can speed up mailings and batch-print long documents, and data base programs can propel your word processing to new accomplishment levels.

If you use a variety of programs frequently, you'll be introduced to methods for making your computer keyboard think it's dedicated to each program you use. There are discussions of utility programs designed to help find files on disks, to move documents from one disk to another, and to organize, organize, organize. There are valuable working hints collected from experienced users.

You'll learn about training programs that teach you how to use other programs and about generating simple graphics to illustrate what you write. You will learn the potential of word processing in conjunction with global communication and research, and about typesetting from your word processor. There's a discussion of ergonomics, the science of adapting equipment and working conditions to meet human needs, and a chapter on word processing as a vocational opportunity.

WORD PROCESSING IS LIKE A SKELETON KEY

Threaded throughout this book is the theme that basic word processing is only the foundation, a springboard to more capabilities. With ingenuity and creative applications, given procedures may be pushed beyond what they are purported to do. "Creative application" will help you use programs more efficiently to arrive at the solutions you need.

Think of a word processing program as a skeleton key. Turn it, place it into other programs to unlock a vast choice of new tools. You'll be like a kid in a store wondering which toy to play with first. You may wish to look at many of them, turn them over, try them, decide which, if any, are exactly right for you. If you're not ready to decide on one today, or tomorrow, it helps to know what's out there so you can grab it when you are ready.

The programs described are meant to serve as an idea of what is on the market and not necessarily a recommendation of one over another. With so much software on the market and a small selection of competitive programs in any one store, it is almost impossible to achieve an overview and comparison of one program against another. Manuals are usually sealed in a shrink wrap. Even if they weren't, unless one can study a program, its commands, and how it gets where it's going, how can an educated judgment be made?

New programs are being introduced constantly. A program will very likely be updated with a new version a few months after it hits the market, and again a few months after that.

By having a comparison basis *before* you buy, you may avoid a wrong, rash, or impulsive purchase. Should you buy a program that doesn't perfectly satisfy your needs, it won't be a total waste. You'll know what you like and don't like. When you evaluate similar programs you'll know what you would want them to do.

Consider each chapter as a reference that you might return to as your word processing needs change and your own expertise matures. Word processors and the operator are like an art medium and an artist. The artist selects his paint, but it takes time to learn to manipulate it. Once familiar with his medium, he can manipulate it as he wants. He begins to search for new brushes, new colors, new tools. A word processing program is the basic medium: all others become the additional tools that help make the art more creative, exciting, and satisfying.

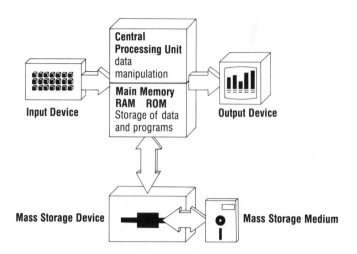

A representation of a simple computer. An input device (keyboard) sends data to the CPU (central processing unit). Data is converted to binary forms which the computer understands, then reconverted, and output in a form that people can understand. Memory (storage area) stores program instructions and data which the CPU manipulates. Output includes the mass storage floppy disk system, and the CRT (cathode ray tube), or terminal.

WORD PROCESSING DEFINED AND HOW IT HAPPENS

If word processing is a new field for you, you will need an overview of the terms used and a basic discussion of the components of a computer system. Those who have systems already may wish to proceed to Chapter 2.

"Word processing" is the manipulation of words on a computer. Basically word processing involves the ability to:

1. *Input* characters into a computer using a keyboard or other input device.
2. *Manipulate* those characters using the capabilities of the computer. "Manipulate" refers to the ability to edit the words, move sentences and paragraphs about on the screen, delete or add characters, then save what you wish to save in the computer's storage device. Usually, it's a floppy disk, but it could be a hard disk or a magnetic tape.
3. *Output* the copy. Output first appears as the words on your CRT (cathode ray tube), or computer terminal screen, also called a VDT (video display terminal). This is where you can read what you input and see what happens as you manipulate it. Another output is a printer with "hard copy" on paper as the result. (If you wish to change a word, phrase, sentence, you can recall the copy from the computer's storage device, correct any portion, then reprint it without having to retype an entire page or document.)

The drawing on page 4 is a graphic representation of a computer system shown in the ITT XTRA.

The usual input device is the keyboard. A "mouse" (at right) is another input device that positions the cursor on the screen, but it is manipulated by hand on a tabletop. The chips and internal hardware reside on "boards" within the case that also houses the disk drive (at right). The terminal and floppy disk storage are output devices.

Photo courtesy of ITT Courier Terminal Systems, Inc.

WHAT YOU WILL NEED

To keep everything clear, let's briefly define what is required to accomplish all this and then cover it in greater depth. The word "computer" has become a catchall term for this whole system that purportedly accomplishes miracles.

Hardware

□ **Microprocessor**—This is a tiny integrated circuit within the computer that is chiefly responsible for transforming or "manipulating" data it receives. With the help of other support chips and software, it also controls the shuttle of information to and from input, output, and storage devices. The computer's internal memory chips store data for immediate access by the microprocessor.

□ **Keyboard**—The keyboard is the device that lets you input, or send commands to the microprocessor. Each time you strike a key, such as an "A" or "B," a special code is sent to the microprocessor. The microprocessor, under control of the word processor or other program you are using, will manipulate, or perform, some meaningful operation on the codes and display the results on the terminal's screen. A "mouse" is another type of input device that can control the cursor's movement on the screen. (The cursor is the symbol that indicates where the next character will appear on the screen.)

☐ **Terminal**—The terminal contains the video screen, which is the output device on which you see the information you input via the keyboard. The appearance of that information on screen may seem instantaneous to you, but before it travels from the keyboard to the terminal it takes a circuitous route over the computer's interior electronics. What happens to the information next? There has to be a way to save it and send it out again in any form you wish.

☐ **External Storage Devices**—The most common storage method for the information is a floppy disk or a hard disk drive. The disk is considered both an input and output device, because information can be either read from it, or recorded to it. The floppy disk is a magnetic receiving medium. It is to the computer system what a tape is to a tape recording system. Some systems do use tape cassettes, but they are less efficient than floppy disks and not very efficient for word processing. Another disk medium is the hard disk; it functions similarly to the floppy disk but stores much more information.

Example of a hard disk storage system. A 5¼-inch Winchester disk has four platters and can store 80 megabytes. In many systems a hard disk replaces one of the floppy disks in a two-drive unit. A hard disk may have one, two, three, or more platters; the more platters the greater the storage capacity and, usually, the faster the retrieval time. Hard disk storage may be backed up with floppy disks or tape storage devices.
Photo courtesy of Computer Memories, Inc.

☐ **Printer**—One more hardware device may be required. A printer, like a terminal and a floppy disk, is an output device. That means it will display the stored information when you are ready to send it out. A printer outputs the data as hard copy—the computer term for written words on paper, compared with copy seen on the terminal screen which will disappear when the computer is turned off.

Software

☐ **Software**—This is an overall term for instructions that tell the computer hardware what to do. A "program" is a specific set of instructions; a "word processing program" consists of instructions that tell the hardware how input characters are to be manipulated. The more detailed and efficient a program, the more capability the computer has to manipulate what is put into it.

WHAT TO CONSIDER WHEN SELECTING A SYSTEM FOR WORD PROCESSING

With so many word processing programs on the market and so many computer systems, selecting the optimum everything is a major research effort.

The following items are part of the total selection process. Offerings swing so pendulumlike that it is helpful to remain flexible about your needs and the system that will serve them best.

Software with the System or Separate? Pros and Cons

Many computer companies include software with their hardware (called bundling) to ease the selection process and to entice a buyer. This has proven such good business practice that some companies have gone even further and developed a word processor that is "resident," or "built into" the system, coordinated with the keyboard—all to make it easier for the user to learn the program.

We have already indicated that one's needs in a word processor program can change. It is quite possible that a program that resides in a system will satisfy all your needs, but if it doesn't, will you be able to change the program?

Another problem. Sometimes programs provided with these systems will not have all the expanded capabilities you'll read about in subsequent chapters: spelling checkers, document sectioning, and others. Will you be able to run separate software with the program given? If not, will such programs be available with that system to accomplish those tasks?

Not so many years ago, and even now, word processing was performed on a word processor—a single-purpose unit. It was "dedicated" only to word processing and no other software could be used on that dedicated machine. The appeal of the microcomputer was that it provided versatility; it could accept instructions from many types of programs. So what happened? Dedicated machines decreased in popularity.

Companies that sold dedicated machines redesigned their hardware so it would offer as much flexibility as a microcomputer.

Now, micro systems are beginning to emulate the dedicated systems with software specifically written for one machine. Beware! Easy learning and no decision making can be a dubious enticement. Be sure you know what you are buying and how flexible it is.

☐ **Choosing a Microprocessor**

The microprocessor, also called the central processing unit (CPU), is often considered the heart and brains of the computer system. The microprocessor your computer uses is an important consideration. Two criteria are important: type and capacity.

The type of microprocessor will often dictate the choices of software available for your system. Selecting a computer with the same microprocessor used on many other popular computers may help to ensure a larger body of compatible software in the marketplace.

The capacity of the microprocessor determines the amount of information that can be manipulated at one time. A *bit*, the smallest measurable unit of data, is also a measure of microprocessor capacity. A 16- or 32-bit microprocessor can manipulate more information at one time and is usually more powerful than an 8-bit microprocessor. Also, 16- or 32-bit microprocessors are designed to more easily control large internal memory storage. Yet an 8-bit machine can be adequate for word processing needs and perform as efficiently with some programs as a machine with a 16- or 32-bit microprocessor.

Another important measurement of data is a *byte*. One byte equals 8 bits. This is roughly the amount of storage required for one character of the alphabet. One kilobyte (K byte) equals just over 1,000 bytes. Disk drive capacity and internal memory capacity are usually expressed in K bytes.

Internal Memory—RAM, ROM

The microcomputer systems you will see—and the word processing programs that may be used in them—refer to sizes such as 64K or 128K or 256K. This measurement has to do with the computer's "internal memory," or RAM (random access memory). RAM memory allows information programs, or data, to be read from or written into it; the speed of access is independent of where the data is located within the memory area. In fact, data input from the disk drive must first be transferred into RAM before it may be accessed by the microprocessor.

To the "end user," the person who uses the program (you) as opposed to the programmer, this means that the bigger the RAM, the more program instructions the microprocessor may read without inefficient and time-consuming transfers between internal and external storage devices.

Some word processing programs require only 48K, but many more require 64K and 128K and some up to 256K. It is logical to assume that a program that requires a 128K system will not work on a machine that has only a 64K RAM capacity.

The disadvantages of RAM? Unlike a floppy disk system, it is "volatile." Anything stored in RAM disappears when the electricity flow stops. But if you asked the computer to send the information in RAM to the floppy disk before you turned off the computer, the information is safe and will be available for future use.

Another type of internal memory is ROM (read only memory). It is similar to RAM except that it is not volatile and its contents may not be changed. It stores programs used frequently; its contents generally are not of great concern to the average user.

How Is External Storage Kept and How Much Information Can Be Held?

The capacity of the external storage device is a major concern and the factor the user interacts with most frequently. The more information a disk can store, the more convenient and time-saving it will be as you work. A disk that can store only 100K bytes on one side will require that you monitor it carefully to be sure you're not trying to stuff more data on it than it will hold (there is a utility that tells you how much of the disk you have used and how much space remains). The less capacity a disk has, the more often you will have to check it, change it, and the more disks you'll have to keep track of, and the less efficient the system will be.

A two-disk drive system is the most convenient setup for word processing, especially if disk capacity is limited. The word processing program will reside on a disk in one drive and the text you write will be developed on the second drive.

How Much Disk Memory Space Do You Need?

A better question is: How much disk space is not enough? Disk space is almost the first thing one outgrows during the writing process. "How much" depends on your personal writing output. If this is your first computer, and word processing will be your major application, avoid the minimum 100K to 125K on a single side, single density 5¼-inch disk. One disk, after some of the system is written, will not even hold 100K.

How does 100K translate into practical terms? 100K is only about 35 pages of double-spaced text on 8½ x 11-inch paper when the copy is printed. If that sounds ample, consider that for each page a second "backup" page is written onto the disk by most programs to ensure against possible loss. That means that the same 100K capacity disk is halved and will store only the equivalent of 18 pages, not enough to hold the first two chapters of this book. Or 20 business letters with addresses for envelopes. One doesn't necessarily store an entire book on one disk at one time, nor is it wise to do so. Working with shorter increments of text, maybe 10 to 30 pages, is wiser and safer; it enables you to move around within a document and from beginning to end faster. But disks that hold too little are inefficient.

A minimal storage capacity system also makes it more difficult to run a document against a spelling program with a large dictionary. It requires disk swapping, which is inconvenient enough to make you avoid using it. If you also want to store long mailing lists, or other data bases, these would have to be broken up into sections alphabetically, or by some other designation, and stored on different disks. For any serious word processing applications, opt for the largest disk capacity system you can afford. If you can't afford the most at once, select a system that can be upgraded to larger capacity at a later date.*

Five and one-quarter- and eight-inch disks are the most popular sizes with 3½-inch disks making headway in the market. Depending on the disk system, disk capacities are expressed as single side single density, single side double density, double side double density, and quad density. If 100K bytes can store about 35 pages of copy, you can estimate how many pages can be stored in larger capacity systems.

Average Disk Storage Capacity

Disk size	Single Density	Double Density	Quad Density
5¼" single sided	100–125K	150–250K	400–500K
5¼" double sided	200–250K	300–500K	800–1000K
8" single sided	240–400K	600–800K	
8" double sided	600–800K	1200–1600K	

How Information Is Written to the Disk

A quick overview of what happens when the computer writes information to the disk will help you understand storage.

A disk is divided into tracks and sectors. The disk controller electronics send signals to move the read/write head to a specific track on the disk. Tracks are arranged as concentric circles on the disk surfaces. Then instructions are sent to either read or write data at that track, while the disk is spun to the correct sector of the track.

Most users won't have to worry about this as the system does it without question—and "transparently," which means that you don't see it happen. You only have to tell the computer what to name each file so it knows how to retrieve it when you want it back again. You might think of the disk as being composed of many file folders and in each is the information you want.

---

* For additional information and in-depth discussion about the technical aspects of computer components and how to evaluate them, refer to the author's earlier volume, *Before You Buy a Computer* (Crown Publishers).

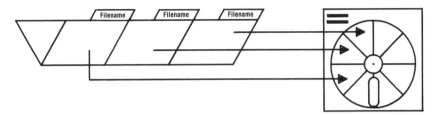

The contents of each file are stored on a sector of the disk. Its file name is written into the directory.

The Key Tronic keyboard has four sections of keys: the standard alphanumeric section, a cursor movement pad, a numeric keypad, and the row of function keys along the top. Some models have all function keys at the left rather than at the top.
Photo courtesy of Key Tronic Corporation

Keyboards and Terminals

The computer keyboard is similar to, but not exactly like, the traditional typewriter keyboard. There are more keys with some dedicated to special functions. There may be arrow keys that will move the cursor up and down and right and left. There will be a control key (CTRL) used in conjunction with a standard key to input a different code to the computer. For example, the "A" by itself will type as an "a"; with a shift key it will type a capital "A." With a control key, it may be used to move the cursor and not produce a character. Different programs will assign different tasks to this combination and to several other control and key combinations. The escape (ESC) key also performs several roles by itself, with other keys. It, too, has differing roles in various programs. An ALT key is another nonprint key that pairs up with other keys.

Most keyboards have a separate numerical keypad at the right that functions the same way as an adding machine or calculator. These keys, too, may be given multiple functions. Many keyboards have additional keys to the left or above the main keyboard and these will be numbered F1 through F10 or F16 depending upon how many there are. There may also be a home key, delete or erase key, a help key or other symbol to designate its function (F is for function).

For the word processing user, a keyboard should be separate from the terminal as opposed to a keyboard and terminal all in one. The keyboard should be able to be placed at a comfortable distance from the screen and the screen itself should be raised, lowered, or tilted to the height requirements of the individual.

How does the keyboard feel? Do the keys spring back quickly? Do they keep up with the speed of the person who is typing the text so that letters don't jumble up? Are the control, function keys, and shift keys in familiar positions so touch typists won't have to readjust constantly? If there is a keyboard key *click,* can it be softened or turned off?

The CRT screen is like the paper on which you write. You have to be able to read it, change it, focus it, alter the light intensity and the relationship of the letters to the background. For word processing, light letters on a dark background are easiest on the eyes. Dark gray with light green or amber characters is preferable to white characters on black background; because of the softer contrast the eyes do not have to read-just as much. Color displays, unless the screen has a very high resolution, cause fuzzy characters that can produce eyestrain. They are not recommended for word processing use over long time periods.

A standard CRT screen will display 80 characters horizontally (normal page width) and 24 or 25 lines vertically so that what you see on screen will simulate the way the text will appear on paper. A screen that displays only 40 or 55 characters horizontally can be disconcerting. Screens that can display a full page (55 lines) vertically are beautiful and may well be worth the extra cost over a 25-line standard display in many work situations.

The size and shape of letters on terminals vary so be sure you are happy with the image presented. You may be looking at that screen for many hours . . . many more than even avid television viewers look at a TV screen, and the image on a terminal does not vary so much. The actual size of the screen merits attention. Generally, a screen that measures 12 inches diagonally, the same size as the average portable TV, will serve most people best. Some portable computers have smaller screens that measure 7 or 9 inches diagonally. The hand-held and lap computers may display only 1, 4, 8, or 16 lines on a liquid crystal display (LCD) or other display technology, but these are not meant for heavy duty word processing. Larger display capacity for such units is predicted for the future.

The CIT 80 monochrome video display terminal and keyboard is a good choice for word processing. The screen displays a standard 25 lines × 80 characters across and yields a sharp image for text. The keyboard has a numerical keypad at right.
Photo courtesy of CIE Terminals, Inc.

The NCR Personal Computer's keyboard is slim and all keys have a round raised area compared with the concave shape of keys on other boards shown.
Photo courtesy of NCR Corporation

A full-page video terminal has a 15-inch vertical monitor that displays 64 lines ×120 characters. Such terminals are higher-priced than standard terminals and will usually interface only with specific systems.
Photo courtesy of CIE Terminals, Inc.

Reverse video or highlighting is a plus feature; both display portions of text as a contrast with other sections. Menus, copy blocks that the user defines for moving about within the document, and misspelled words, will stand out more than if they are designated only with a cursor.

COMPATIBILITY

Not all programs work on all machines. If you decide on a program that you like before you buy a computer, be sure it is compatible with the disk operating system (DOS) of the computer and that the computer you buy has ample RAM to accommodate the program. If you already have a system, you are committed to a program that will work with it and your choice may be limited. Each program should be carefully evaluated by consulting charts and comparing notes with other people in a computer society or user group. Determine if the dealer from whom you buy a program will provide support or a training session and if the software company will be available for telephone questions. If no one you know is using the program yet, think twice about being a pioneer. When word processing is new to you, you may have a struggle and no one with whom to compare notes.

TRY BEFORE YOU BUY

When possible, spend many hours working with a system and a program before you buy *anything*. Don't hesitate to return to a salesroom, sit down in front of a system with demonstration software, and ask the salesperson questions. Ask yourself questions, too, the same ones posed above. A salesperson won't *know* how the keyboard feels to you. Take a class or a training session, or work with a friend's system. Users' groups often hold work sessions in schools where terminals and software are available. That way, you'll have some basis for comparison, an insight into your own comfort levels, your own likes and dislikes about a system, and how it feels. You'll be able to learn more by watching what other people are doing, too.

HOW PORTABLE?

Another choice may involve the size of the computer for your word processing needs. Portability becomes a factor for many people. There are increasingly greater selections of portable computers that will handle word processing.

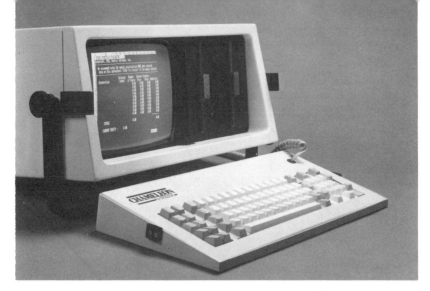

The Chameleon by Seequa is a suitcase-size portable computer with two floppy disk drives, a detachable keyboard, and a 9-inch horizontally measured CRT. It is a full-function 16-bit machine that runs IBM PC compatible software.
Photo courtesy of Seequa Computer Corporation

Lap computers may change the way many people use word processing. The new portables often have the word processing program on a chip in read-only-memory. Documents prepared while away from the office may be moved to a desk top machine or printed directly from the lap computer with a special printer. The Hewlett-Packard Portable has a built-in 80-character by 16-line liquid crystal display which swivels to any viewing angle. A 3½-inch disk drive is optional. The system is powered by battery and AC adapter.
Courtesy of Hewlett-Packard Corp.

Portability and big machine are offered by the Apricot Computer, which is 16-bit PCDOS AND MSDOS compatible. The company is promoting the idea of having two display terminals, perhaps one at home and one at the office. The user has to transport only the computer, drive, and keyboard, which pack into a compact carrying case. The keyboard also has a one-line LCD (liquid crystal display) that can substitute for the large display as a temporary viewing output. The Apricot uses a 3½-inch disk system. It also contains an interior modem.
Photo courtesy of ACT (North America), Inc.

Lap-size units can display enough lines of text and sophistication for limited use when traveling. The text could then be transferred to a conventional unit for further manipulation and/or storage on a disk using disk transfer procedures or a data transfer with a modem.

Briefcase- and suitcase-size portables usually can accept the same range and assortment of compatible software as their big brother counterparts. They may have smaller screens. Some may lack expansion potential within the unit for adding memory or boards to increase capabilities. There may be some sacrifice in speed and in the quality of a keyboard, depending upon the unit and its price. But for word processing they can yield the same results.

2. Word Processing —Fantasy and Reality

Until you spend time using a word processing program, everything you are told seems miraculous, effortless, work-free—a dream. A fantasy. Is it possible that typewriting has evolved into this incredible ability? Yes, you can create copy by moving words and paragraphs, deleting, inserting, spelling and punctuating correctly, and see a finished document impeccably formatted before it is committed to paper.

But don't get carried away. There still is no Santa Claus. The computer and the software are remarkable. They remove mountains of monotony, relieve typing and retyping tedium. The ride is easier, but it's not free. Neither is the vehicle perfect; nor are problems forever banished.

Word processing could be compared to the automobile. It needs gas and you to run it and it sure beats walking. But some cars are better than others, some more expensive, more comfortable, and pleasanter to drive.

The computer needs software and you to run it and it beats typing. But all computers and software are not created equal. Some have more "accessories" and are more elegant. Conversely, some are so downright clumsy that if they were a car, they wouldn't be worth gassing up unless you were driving them to the junk heap, and they might clunk and lose parts on the way.

The number, type, and power of the tools in a basic word processing program can vary tremendously. A simple program with minimal features may be adequate for someone who writes only a few letters a month and won't remember sophisticated procedures and complex commands. Most people who look at word processing for serious output, business applications, book and report generation, research, class work, and more, will seek power and the tools to facilitate the work.

But power and tools are not the only considerations. When one compares reference cards from several programs, some may have more features listed, more commands. Is more better? Not necessarily. There's an almost ethereal element that defies charting. It is **elegance and grace** compared to **awkwardness and clumsiness.**

There are programs that appear to be utopia if one judges by the advertising, manuals, and reference cards. Nothing seems to be lacking. Except elegance and grace—and that never shows until you spend time with them. They are clumsy, awkward, inelegant. Like an elephant trying to perform *Swan Lake.*

Programs differ in these qualities. One program may have elegant editing features, but formatting requires extra steps. If one format command is wrong you might spend hours finding the culprit, correcting it in the file, and reformatting.

A reference card may indicate that one program has twice as many cursor control commands as another. Wow! You can move in so many increments—more than in a comparably priced program for the same system. But that program requires that you shift "modes" when you want to add copy and when you want to delete a character, word, or other text. It's like shifting gears in a car. You must stop before you can shift into reverse and shift again to go forward. If you're typing and decide to go back to delete a character, you have to shift into the "backward" mode, then the "insert" mode, then again into the "forward" mode. To add in one character, you may have to strike as many as 5 or 6 keys and remember the order needed!

And menus! You'll see many references to "menu oriented" programs that simplify the procedures. That's fine. At the beginning. But later, when you know the procedures and where you want to go, you no longer need menus cluttering up your screen. There should be a way to eliminate them!

How can you tell when a program is inelegant, clumsy? How do you know when a theatrical performance is poorly done? It takes time to cultivate taste; it requires exposure to the medium to know what is good and what is bad, what you like and don't like. You almost have to know one word processing program before you can differentiate between virtues and flaws. How can you begin?

1. Establish some parameters, some goals for developing your personal tastes on how a word processor performs.
2. Decide the features you want a program to have and how you wish they could be accomplished.
3. Determine the features you don't need.
4. Determine features about which you are neutral.

5. Make your own "benchmark" or set of standards by which you will judge a program.

Programs may be listed in a current computer magazine with a series of yeses and noes about their features. Such charts are a big help, but they show only what a program does, not how gracefully it works. Another procedure? Establish one or two series of moves that you feel are important and measure each program against those. Here are some ideas to spark your thinking:

1. Does the program offer a *list of your files* on the disk? Are they randomly sorted or are they alphabetized? (Alphabetized files are easier to locate.) Is the appearance of the file optional? (It takes longer to list a file and when you don't need it, you should be able to turn it off.)
2. Start a "keystroke test." Select one semicomplex, but standard, function and compare the *number of keystrokes* required to accomplish it. How many keys must be actually hit to define a block of copy and move it to a new place? One test that compared this feature in three programs revealed 24 keystrokes for one program, 35 for another, and 14 for a third.
3. How complex, and how foolproof, are the *commands for saving a file?* Are files backed up automatically? Must you write the file name every time you want to save it? Or will the program remember the last entry typed? When a program remembers, it's safer. There's danger in having to retype a name every time you want to save a file. You could mistype and have two copies saved under two names. Do this a couple of times and files will multiply like rabbits. You won't know which one you did what with.

It isn't easy to establish a meaningful rating scale for "elegance." Only some portions of a program may be clumsy. What portions will you have to forgive? Are you willing to do so?

Specific examples:

WordStar lets you delete copy, but it does not allow you to retrieve it, or "undelete." That's a clumsy feature. But WordStar's formatting features are graceful.

Perfect Writer's split screen capability, a feature that enables the user to see and edit two files simultaneously, is elegant. But the same program has clumsy procedures for formatting a document.

If you have to stop printing a document to correct it, can you reprint from the cursor position? From the beginning of a page? Printing procedures can be incredibly clumsy on otherwise graceful programs.

Programs written specifically for the 16-bit MSDOS and PCDOS systems have added a broader dimension to word processing compared with 8-bit systems. Many programs are emulating dedicated machines, yet they can be used on different computers with the same operating system. They may require more than 64K memory to run: 128K or 192K or 256K bytes. Some programs may not accept a stand alone spelling checker, or a thesaurus, and if such programs are not available from the same program series, you may be limiting your computer's capability.

LEARNING HOW TO USE A PROGRAM

Word processing programs require learning many new sets of commands. Software companies are trying hard to simplify the procedures and to provide training that facilitates the learning process. But selecting a program mainly because it is easy to learn can be a mistake. Sometimes, the easier a program is to learn, the fewer commands, the less it can do. Manuals and documentation are improving. Consider that the learning process may take only a few weeks, but you'll use the program for a long time. You don't have to learn it all at once.

YOUR PERSONAL CHECK LIST

Each of the features in the following list is within the capability of word processing. The list is a combination of features in many programs; none have every one. Study the list and read the description of what each feature accomplishes in the following text. If you plan to test several programs, photocopy several sheets so you can profile one program on each sheet and check the boxes that apply to each program.

With the same information gathered for several programs you'll soon have an insight into your needs, desires, and which programs offer the most features you want.

Comparison lists of word processors appear in current magazines regularly. The programs change so frequently, with more features added, that any list is out of date almost as soon as it appears. With so many available for different machines, a comprehensive list would be prohibitive spacewise. You will learn more about word processing by compiling your personal word processing profile.

Computer and software purchases are the best argument for the old caution: *Caveat emptor.* Let the buyer beware. For any entry where you check "do not understand," do your homework until you do understand. Item entry explanations follow.

The list may appear formidable. But not every person needs all the features. Statistics indicate that most people use only about 20 percent of a program's capabilities. If you aim for the sky, you may not need it, or use it. Yet it's nice to know it's there if and when you want it.

YOUR PERSONAL WORD PROCESSING PROGRAM PROFILE

1. Overall Considerations

Name of program _____

Company _____

DOS _____

Kind of machine needed _____

No. of kilobytes required _____

Disk size available, 5¼″ or 8″ _____

Backup/copy protection policy _____

Price _____

	Do not understand	Must have	Neutral	Not essential
2. Documentation				
On disk	[ ]	[ ]	[ ]	[ ]
On tape	[ ]	[ ]	[ ]	[ ]
Reference manual	[ ]	[ ]	[ ]	[ ]
with table of contents	[ ]	[ ]	[ ]	[ ]
with index	[ ]	[ ]	[ ]	[ ]
Quick reference card	[ ]	[ ]	[ ]	[ ]
Paste-on key tabs	[ ]	[ ]	[ ]	[ ]
Keyboard templates	[ ]	[ ]	[ ]	[ ]
3. Menus				
Can they be turned on/off?	[ ]	[ ]	[ ]	[ ]
How many are there?	[ ]	[ ]	[ ]	[ ]
4. Cursor Control				
By character	[ ]	[ ]	[ ]	[ ]
By word	[ ]	[ ]	[ ]	[ ]
By beginning and end of sentence	[ ]	[ ]	[ ]	[ ]
By beginning and end of paragraph	[ ]	[ ]	[ ]	[ ]
By given number of characters/lines	[ ]	[ ]	[ ]	[ ]
By top and bottom of screen	[ ]	[ ]	[ ]	[ ]
By jumping to page/line	[ ]	[ ]	[ ]	[ ]
By top and bottom of document	[ ]	[ ]	[ ]	[ ]
Ability to set/jump to markers	[ ]	[ ]	[ ]	[ ]
Ability to convert cases/All cap/lc	[ ]	[ ]	[ ]	[ ]
5. Delete Control				
Necessary to shift modes?	[ ]	[ ]	[ ]	[ ]
By character	[ ]	[ ]	[ ]	[ ]
By word	[ ]	[ ]	[ ]	[ ]
By line	[ ]	[ ]	[ ]	[ ]
From cursor to beginning of line	[ ]	[ ]	[ ]	[ ]
From cursor to end of line	[ ]	[ ]	[ ]	[ ]
By sentence	[ ]	[ ]	[ ]	[ ]
By paragraph	[ ]	[ ]	[ ]	[ ]

	Do not understand	Must have	Neutral	Not essential
By screen	[ ]	[ ]	[ ]	[ ]
By block	[ ]	[ ]	[ ]	[ ]
By given number of lines/characters	[ ]	[ ]	[ ]	[ ]
By repeat key for continuous delete	[ ]	[ ]	[ ]	[ ]
Ability to retrieve deleted copy	[ ]	[ ]	[ ]	[ ]

6. Insert

	Do not understand	Must have	Neutral	Not essential
Change modes	[ ]	[ ]	[ ]	[ ]
Insert character	[ ]	[ ]	[ ]	[ ]
Insert lines	[ ]	[ ]	[ ]	[ ]
Necessary to open text first?	[ ]	[ ]	[ ]	[ ]
Another file into current text?	[ ]	[ ]	[ ]	[ ]

7. Scrolling

	Do not understand	Must have	Neutral	Not essential
By full screen up and down	[ ]	[ ]	[ ]	[ ]
By half screen up and down	[ ]	[ ]	[ ]	[ ]
Horizontal scroll to n characters	[ ]	[ ]	[ ]	[ ]

8. Search

	Do not understand	Must have	Neutral	Not essential
Find character/word/string	[ ]	[ ]	[ ]	[ ]
Find and replace n times	[ ]	[ ]	[ ]	[ ]
Find and replace but ask first	[ ]	[ ]	[ ]	[ ]
Find and replace all occurrences	[ ]	[ ]	[ ]	[ ]
Ignore upper/lower case	[ ]	[ ]	[ ]	[ ]
Find and replace backward	[ ]	[ ]	[	[ ]
Use wild cards	[ ]	[ ]	[ ]	[ ]

9. Screen Display

	Do not understand	Must have	Neutral	Not essential
What you see is what you get —text underlines, boldface, italics	[ ]	[ ]	[ ]	[ ]
Menu driven	[ ]	[ ]	[ ]	[ ]
Continuous status information page, line, col., characters	[ ]	[ ]	[ ]	[ ]
Automatic page break	[ ]	[ ]	[ ]	[ ]
Ability to hide/display controls	[ ]	[ ]	[ ]	[ ]
Windowing capability	[ ]	[ ]	[ ]	[ ]
Editing multiple documents	[ ]	[ ]	[ ]	[ ]
Mouse selection capability	[ ]	[ ]	[ ]	[ ]

10. Text Control

	Do not understand	Must have	Neutral	Not essential
Justify right margin	[ ]	[ ]	[ ]	[ ]
Justify left margin	[ ]	[ ]	[ ]	[ ]
Center text	[ ]	[ ]	[ ]	[ ]
Reformatting by paragraphs	[ ]	[ ]	[ ]	[ ]
Reformatting automatically	[ ]	[ ]	[ ]	[ ]
Margin control	[ ]	[ ]	[ ]	[ ]
Block moves horizontally	[ ]	[ ]	[ ]	[ ]
Block moves by columns	[ ]	[ ]	[ ]	[ ]

	Do not understand	Must have	Neutral	Not essential
Copy blocks	[ ]	[ ]	[ ]	[ ]
Move blocks	[ ]	[ ]	[ ]	[ ]
Pick up multiple blocks	[ ]	[ ]	[ ]	[ ]
Style forms for document design	[ ]	[ ]	[ ]	[ ]
See what you get	[ ]	[ ]	[ ]	[ ]
Use special formatting commands	[ ]	[ ]	[ ]	[ ]
Automatic word wrap on/off	[ ]	[ ]	[ ]	[ ]
Automatic hyphenation on/off	[ ]	[ ]	[ ]	[ ]

11. Page Design Control

	Do not understand	Must have	Neutral	Not essential
Set/clear tabs	[ ]	[ ]	[ ]	[ ]
Set margins left and right	[ ]	[ ]	[ ]	[ ]
Change page length	[ ]	[ ]	[ ]	[ ]
Change head/foot margins	[ ]	[ ]	[ ]	[ ]
Change character pitch	[ ]	[ ]	[ ]	[ ]
Change no. of lines per inch	[ ]	[ ]	[ ]	[ ]
One-line headings	[ ]	[ ]	[ ]	[ ]
Two-line headings	[ ]	[ ]	[ ]	[ ]
One-line footings	[ ]	[ ]	[ ]	[ ]
Two-line footings	[ ]	[ ]	[ ]	[ ]
Change position of headings/footings	[ ]	[ ]	[ ]	[ ]
Automatic page numbering	[ ]	[ ]	[ ]	[ ]
Begin at a page other than 1	[ ]	[ ]	[ ]	[ ]
Turn off page numbering	[ ]	[ ]	[ ]	[ ]
Place page no. in head/foot	[ ]	[ ]	[ ]	[ ]
Reference numbers to another page	[ ]	[ ]	[ ]	[ ]
Footnotes, endnotes	[ ]	[ ]	[ ]	[ ]
Eliminate widows and orphans	[ ]	[ ]	[ ]	[ ]

12. File Handling

	Do not understand	Must have	Neutral	Not essential
File directory on/off	[ ]	[ ]	[ ]	[ ]
Alphabetized?	[ ]	[ ]	[ ]	[ ]
Can files be	[ ]	[ ]	[ ]	[ ]
written to another file?	[ ]	[ ]	[ ]	[ ]
retrieved from another file?	[ ]	[ ]	[ ]	[ ]
deleted when in a different file?	[ ]	[ ]	[ ]	[ ]
Automatically backed up when saved	[ ]	[ ]	[ ]	[ ]
Save file and continue edit	[ ]	[ ]	[ ]	[ ]
Delete file	[ ]	[ ]	[ ]	[ ]
Merge file	[ ]	[ ]	[ ]	[ ]
Copy a single file	[ ]	[ ]	[ ]	[ ]
Delete a single file	[ ]	[ ]	[ ]	[ ]
Rename a file	[ ]	[ ]	[ ]	[ ]
Nondocument files	[ ]	[ ]	[ ]	[ ]
Disk status	[ ]	[ ]	[ ]	[ ]

	Do not understand	Must have	Neutral	Not essential
13. Printing				
Format before printing?	[ ]	[ ]	[ ]	[ ]
Underline	[ ]	[ ]	[ ]	[ ]
Boldface	[ ]	[ ]	[ ]	[ ]
Subscript and superscript	[ ]	[ ]	[ ]	[ ]
Overtype	[ ]	[ ]	[ ]	[ ]
Proportional spacing	[ ]	[ ]	[ ]	[ ]
Interrupt/resume printing	[ ]	[ ]	[ ]	[ ]
Pause for text entry	[ ]	[ ]	[ ]	[ ]
Pause to change type element	[ ]	[ ]	[ ]	[ ]
Print multiple copies	[ ]	[ ]	[ ]	[ ]
Stop print between pages	[ ]	[ ]	[ ]	[ ]
Include another file	[ ]	[ ]	[ ]	[ ]
Batch files	[ ]	[ ]	[ ]	[ ]
Print one file/edit another	[ ]	[ ]	[ ]	[ ]
Convert to all upper or lower case	[ ]	[ ]	[ ]	[ ]
14. Enhancements				
Mail merge included	[ ]	[ ]	[ ]	[ ]
Mail merge program extra	[ ]	[ ]	[ ]	[ ]
Spelling program included	[ ]	[ ]	[ ]	[ ]
Spelling program available	[ ]	[ ]	[ ]	[ ]
Other spelling program applicable	[ ]	[ ]	[ ]	[ ]
Sectioning long documents	[ ]	[ ]	[ ]	[ ]
table of contents	[ ]	[ ]	[ ]	[ ]
index (no. of levels)	[ ]	[ ]	[ ]	[ ]
Ability to change format	[ ]	[ ]	[ ]	[ ]
Thesaurus	[ ]	[ ]	[ ]	[ ]
Math program	[ ]	[ ]	[ ]	[ ]
Word count	[ ]	[ ]	[ ]	[ ]
Page count	[ ]	[ ]	[ ]	[ ]
Form letter generator	[ ]	[ ]	[ ]	[ ]
15. Other				
Ability to change defaults easily	[ ]	[ ]	[ ]	[ ]
Takes advantage of function keys	[ ]	[ ]	[ ]	[ ]
Macros for redefining keys	[ ]	[ ]	[ ]	[ ]
Modem communication	[ ]	[ ]	[ ]	[ ]
Business graphics capability	[ ]	[ ]	[ ]	[ ]
Line drawing capability	[ ]	[ ]	[ ]	[ ]
_____	[ ]	[ ]	[ ]	[ ]
_____	[ ]	[ ]	[ ]	[ ]

16. Keystroke Test Result

Feature used for test _____

Number of strokes required _____

ANALYZING THE LIST

The following explanations will help to clarify each of the entries in the profile list.

1. Overall Considerations

Early in your research you'll realize that the names of many programs are similar. After you investigate a few they may all begin to melt into a whirl of sameness. Word, WordStar, Perfect Writer, Easy Writer II, Word II, The FinalWord. Some, in an effort to capture the market's attention, will have names that defy association with word processing: Benchmark, Palantir, Blue, MultiMate, Leading Edge, PowerText, and so on.

How can you sort them out? Make one check list for each program you consider. Tear out an ad for the program from a magazine, or attach a brochure. Brochures will be available by filling out the information cards in the back of a magazine, or from a dealer. Record the name of the company, too. When you request references from other users, you'll want to know how that company supports the product. You'll have to know the disk operating system and the kind of machine on which the program will or will not run. Some programs are only for 16-bit PCDOS compatibility machines, others for CP/M DOS, APPLE DOS, TRS-80 DOS, etc. The number of kilobytes is important, too. A 48K Apple disk operating system will not run a 64K CP/M program or a 192K MSDOS program. Be sure the program is supplied with the size disks that will fit in your disk drives.

Many programs are "copy protected." This policy may limit the number of working copies you can have. It may require that you send the original to the company for a backup, a waste of your time when you buy a program that you want to begin using immediately. Protection methods vary. Be sure you know what they are for any program and how the policy may limit its use for your purposes.

Check prices carefully. A program will often sell for less than its list price and that discounted price can vary by dealers and by mail order companies.

2. Documentation

A program may contain a tutorial on disk. (If a tutorial is available only from a third-party dealer, it will cost extra.) Some companies market training aids on a videotape or on a tape recorder so the lesson applies to any computer system regardless of disk size or DOS.

A manual is a must and it should be complete with a table of contents and index. A sloppy manual may indicate a sloppy program, although not always. Sometimes a beautiful manual disguises a sloppy program.

Quick reference cards, keyboard overlays, stick-on key tops, and templates are aids for using and learning which keys perform different commands in a specific program.

Help menus in a word processing program can take up too much of the screen. The program should let you retain a menu on screen if needed, delete it when not needed, and call it back when necessary. A help menu from the popular program WordStar by MicroPro is displayed on the terminal of a Monroe System 2000 16-bit microcomputer system. WordStar has one of the best help menu plans on the market because it can be removed and displayed readily.

Photo courtesy of Monroe Systems for Business

Many programs have a quick reference card listing the commands, and a set of paste-on key tabs for the keyboard. Some have printed templates. There may be a blank template so you can identify any keys you give a new definition to with a macro (described in Chapter 12). These are handy, but their absence or presence should not be a deciding factor.

3. Menus

Programs that are menu-oriented supply on-screen lists so you can select the action you must take to proceed: edit a file, delete a file, move the cursor, select margins, etc. These are fine when you're a beginner, but they may take up screen space and take time to appear. That can slow up the procedure. When you no longer need them, you should be able to elect whether you want to view them.

The help menus in the program Word Right are comprehensive and easy to bring on screen when you need help. Hit one key to bring up the list of commands; that list provides the keys needed to perform a function. If you need help for that function, a help key is combined with the necessary letter and a complete explanation appears on screen.

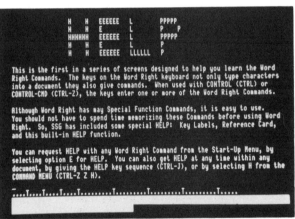

```
(Perfect Writer) Perfect Formatter Selection Menu
(C) 1982 Perfect Software, Inc.

    Available options for the formatter are:
        C - Send the output to the console device
        D - Format for a different device type
        P - Send the output to the printer device
        O - Name the output file differently
        V - Make the top level environment Verbatim instead of Text
            (Verbatim causes the output to appear as it does on the screen)
        A - Pause for manual insertion of each sheet of paper
        G - Start the formatting now
        X - Return to the top level of the menu




pf
Your pleasure: (D, C, P, O, V, A, G, X) D
What device do you wish to format this for? a_
```

```
Perfect Writer Version 1.03 Main Selection Menu
(C) 1982 Perfect Software, Inc.

    Selections:
        E - Edit a file                           (pw)
        F - Format a file                         (pf)
        P - Print a formatted file                (pp)
        S - Check the spelling of a file          (ps)

        D - Look at the directory on a disk
        Z - Delete (erase) a file
        R - Rename a file

        C - Send a command line to CP/M
        X - Exit from this menu to CP/M




Type one character to indicate your selection now.
Your pleasure: (E, F, P, S, D, Z, R, C, X) E
What is the name of the file you wish to edit?
)B:chisord.pro_
```

Perfect Writer's edit menu provides a list of editing procedures. A second menu controls the formatting. A third menu (not shown) brings in the printing choices. Selections are made from all menus to accomplish an edit, to format, and to print.

Many menus may be convenient but they can also be overdone. One program has 14 menus that prompt you every step of the process from the second you call up the program until you are through printing. None can be skipped or deleted. That's an inflexible, inelegant process.

4. Cursor Control

Despite the presence, or absence, of all other features considered, the ability to move the cursor quickly around the screen is probably the most critical feature in any program. Minimal automatic cursor positioning will slow up your work more than any other characteristic. Every program will let you move a character at a time, but other increments are not always available. The more increments of movements available, the more versatile the movement—if you employ them all.

BASIC EDITING

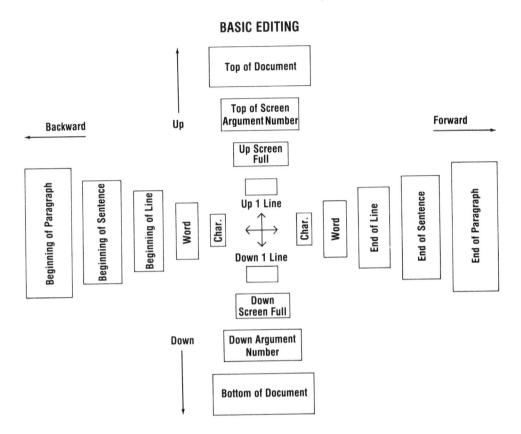

Perfect Writer offers comprehensive cursor control movement commands; character, beginning and end of word, beginning and end of line, of sentence, of paragraph; up and down one line, screenful, top and bottom of document. Any "number" can be selected with each command and the cursor will move by that number.

It is with this basic requirement that incredible clumsiness occurs in many programs. Having the capability to move the cursor back and forth or up and down quickly is only good if it is accomplished with minimal commands *and* integrated with the delete movements.

This is where one should consider, and be wary of, the mode concept. A good program will let you shift from cursor to delete movement with only one or two commands. If a program has you shifting modes before you can delete or return to adding characters, it is clumsy.

Few programs jump about by every increment in the list. How will you know which programs have what? A good clue as to the thoroughness of cursor movements is to look at the prompt card or summary of prompts in the manual and check them against the list.

Setting markers refers to a feature that lets you establish a spot in the text, move about and do other things, then hit a key to return you to that marker immediately. Some programs can set as many as ten markers. When the feature does not exist, it can be improvised by setting any strange combination of letters in the text, and using the search feature to return to the strange letters.

Being able to convert any amount of text from caps to lower case and vise versa, and requesting that only the first letter of each word be capitalized is rare, but it should be deemed standard. Think of how often you type a line and then decide it should be all capitals, or caps and lower case, or all lower case. When the program won't do it, you have to retype each character to be changed.

5. Delete Control

The same conditions that apply to cursor control apply to delete capabilities with one major addition. If you accidentally, or purposely, delete a portion of text, can you retrieve it? Or has it gone to oblivion so you have to reenter it if you want it back? That's clumsy. Programs usually give this retrieve capability a "cutesy" name such as "oops," "yankback," "goof," "undelete," etc.

6. Insert

How convenient is it to insert copy? If it requires a mode change, it's inelegant. If it requires a concerted move to open the text, bring in the insert, and then close it, it's clumsy.

Can you bring in another file and insert it into the document on which you are currently working? That's essential.

7. Scrolling

Scrolling refers to the ability to move text up and down the screen quickly. The average screen displays 24 lines of text; would you like to be able to move the whole screen at a time? Half a screen? Up, then back down? Would you like to have one or two lines from the previous screen remain at the top or bottom so you have some text for continuity? How many options are there for scrolling? Can it be accomplished smoothly and not jump a screen at a time? Can the scroll be controlled to move faster or slower so you can read it or scan it quickly?

A horizontal scroll is a good feature should you wish to type lines longer than the average 65 characters and still see how the lines will appear. How many characters across will be scrolled?

8. Search

Once you've discovered the versatility of the tools "search" and "search and replace," you'll realize that such conveniences are never possible with a typewriter. A flexible program will let you select a variety of combinations for a search routine—a character, a word, or several words, referred to as a "string."

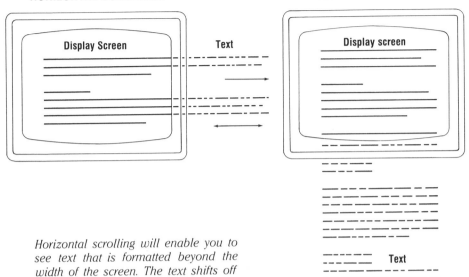

HORIZONTAL SCROLLING

VERTICAL SCROLLING

Horizontal scrolling will enable you to see text that is formatted beyond the width of the screen. The text shifts off screen to the left, but it isn't lost.

Vertical scrolling should be accomplished by screenful, by line, by half-screen, and a continuous scroll with a control for speed usually accomplished by using a number: 1 is fastest and it slows through 10.

"Search" alone will look for every occurrence of a string in the text and you make the correction.

"Search and replace" will look for every occurrence of a string and then exchange, add, delete another string automatically. It should provide several options: request that a string be replaced x number of times, or throughout the entire file without stopping, or stop each time it finds the string and let you decide what to do. It should offer a "wild card" search using a question mark, or other symbol, to represent a character that could differ within the string it is searching for. Whole-word-only search is handy. Should you look for the letter combination "oo" only, you would be stopped at every word that had "oo"s within, such as "book," "took," "too." A whole-word search requests that only these letters used as a word would be found.

Can you reverse search movement and proceed from top to bottom and bottom to top of the text?

9. Screen Display

"What you see is what you get" (explained below under Text Control) also applies to underlines, boldface, and similar instructions to the printer. Do they appear as you would see them printed in text? Must they be enclosed between commands?

If menus do appear on screen, how legible are they? How much do they interfere with text input? If your terminal supports reverse video or highlighting, will the program take advantage of that feature?

Is there a status line on screen as you work, or can you call it up instantly for a report on the amount of text you have input? Can you learn instantly where you are in the document by line, column, number of characters, page? If the information is on screen, can it be turned off?

Does the screen show where the end of page will appear? One problem with programs that do not show automatic page breaks is that you may print a document and discover that a chapter or subhead title is the last line on a page and there is no easy way to circumvent that. Such programs may offer the option to view a formatted copy of the text on screen or place a copy in another file for previewing before it is printed. That means returning to the file, fixing it, unformatting. Then subsequent pages will change.

Commands for print controls (see Printing below) often require that control characters be placed before and after the string of text. For example ^PS will result in underlining the text between the two ^PS commands. This will cause the actual text on screen to appear out of format. Can you turn off and "hide" these commands so you can see exactly how the formatted text will appear?

Split screen or window capability lets you see two or more files on screen simultaneously. With multiple file editing, different files may be called in during an edit though only two may be viewed at the same time.

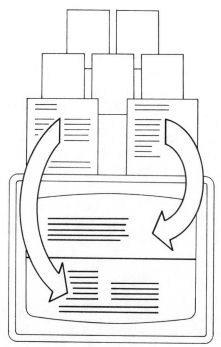

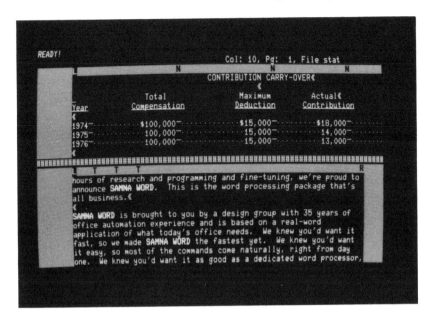

An illustration of two programs seen with a split screen editing capability with the Samna Word. The bottom screen has text for word processing while the top screen shows a spreadsheet. The lighter borders indicate the current margin settings. The cursor can jump to either screen. Any function that can be accomplished with a single screen can also be done in each screen.

Courtesy of Samna Corporation

"Window" permits several files and types of programs to appear simultaneously.

Courtesy of Corvus Systems

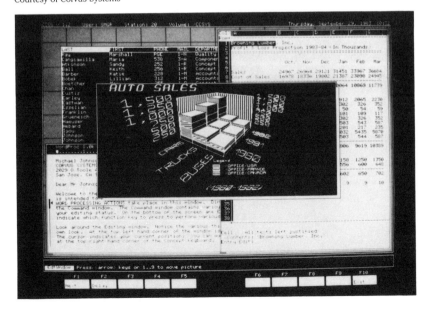

A mouse is an input device that controls the cursor. The unit is moved across the desktop with your hand and the direction of the mouse controls the direction of the cursor. Top controls simulate the entry key on the keyboard.
Photo courtesy of Key Tronic Corporation

Several programs have split-screen capabilities which permit viewing and editing two documents on screen simultaneously. *Windowing* permits multiple documents to be placed on the screen simultaneously. The screen actually appears as a set of rectangles or squares and information within each area can be manipulated individually.

Some programs will accept input from a mouse or other device in addition to the keyboard. A mouse can't enter alphanumerics, but it can indicate, by cursor or highlighting, where to open space for character or line insertions, to define blocks, when to reformat, and which selection to make from a menu. A button on top of the mouse is pressed and emulates the return key on the keyboard. The program and the hardware must be able to support the device.

10. Text Control

Most programs provide the capability of having the right margin justified or not justified, but not all programs show on screen exactly how the lines will break when printed. Sometimes a program will allow you to justify the left margin, a nice feature when typing columns or arranging a specially designed layout.

Almost all have features for centering a line of text, reformatting, and setting margins. But the gracefulness of margin sets and related changes in page format can vary considerably. This is one area you should investigate carefully if you change page formatting frequently.

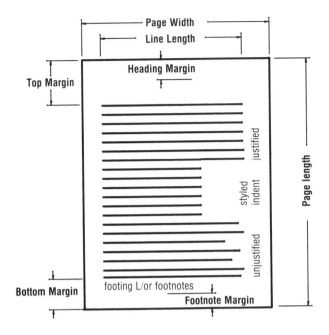

All word processing programs enable you to design a page by altering the main margins, top, bottom, and sides. Text can be justified so lines are even at the right margin, or unjustified so they are ragged. With some programs it is difficult to retain a section of text that you want formatted differently—and that can be frustrating. Page numbering, header and footer margins, and the number of lines should be flexible.

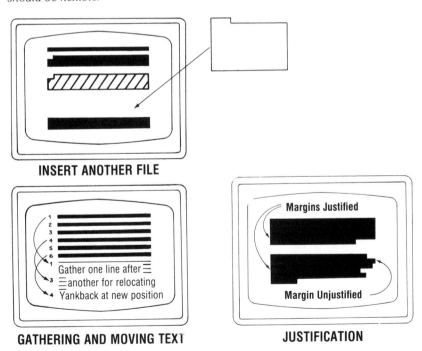

INSERT ANOTHER FILE

GATHERING AND MOVING TEXT

JUSTIFICATION

MOVE A COLUMN

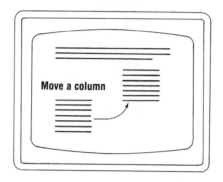

Some programs have formatting procedures that are so painful that a trip to the dentist might seem like a game. Formatting may be accomplished by requesting it for each paragraph or through an entire document. Newer programs may reform paragraphs automatically whenever character entries change the length of a line. That sounds good, but too much of it may also make you dizzy.

A block move is the capability of defining a block of text at the beginning and end and moving it elsewhere in the document or to a new file. Most programs do it, but some are cumbersome and slow with a tendency to lose the block somewhere in the transition. Many require so many commands to accomplish the task you might think you're moving the Rock of Gibraltar.

Defining a column and moving it is a sophisticated procedure that was a rarity rather than the norm in early programs. Newer programs almost always include it.

Once a block is defined, it should be able to be copied as many times as you like. You should be able to delete it from one place and put it into another (usually called cut and paste).

Generally, a program will allow you to define one block and deal with it. If you wish to pick up a second block of copy, you have to redo the entire procedure. Will a program gather up one bit of text after another, like lint on a couch, and let you combine it into another block for placement elsewhere? How many characters of text can be picked each time?

Preset style forms for specific layouts are offered in many programs and their use is optional. This means you type copy in any random fashion. Just before and immediately after a specific portion of text, you enter a style code that the printer knows to put into that format.

A "style format" may be a two-level outline, a business letter, a salutation. It's not quite as simple as it sounds; you still have to learn other directives. But it can be an advantageous feature if you don't mind using a series of special formatting commands and not being able to view the output on screen.

The most popular programs are those that let you see, on screen, exactly the way the copy will appear when printed. Page breaks are designated, copy is formatted in lines, paragraphs, pages, so that what you see is what you get.

The alternative procedure involves using special formatting commands at the top or within the file. Copy is input in a relatively informal placement. It doesn't matter if you delete a portion of a line and leave a blank space, the hard copy will have it all printed neatly. If you wish copy double-spaced, you place the command at the top and any single-spaced entered copy will be double-spaced when printed.

One of the beauties of word processing is that words wrap automatically at the end of the line, but in some cases this may not be desired. Can it be turned off? And the same question applies to automatic hyphenation, which sounds like a good feature. But if reformatting is required, that hyphenated word may fall in the center of a line and you will have to delete the hyphen. If these features are defaults (preset by the program), can the user override the defaults when desired? That should be very high on your wish list. You may not realize how important it is until you work with word processing for a while.

11. Page Design Control

Can tabs be cleared and reset conveniently and will they hold throughout the entire edit? Can a single tab be set and cleared quickly?

Resetting margins for an entire document as well as within a document would be expected, but not all programs can do both and do them with equal grace. It may be possible to request that an entire document appear with certain margins, but to establish a different margin for a portion within that text will be difficult when reformatting occurs. If you establish narrow margins within a document manually, then reform the entire piece, will the format be lost? Or retained? You should be able to change the amount of space at the top and bottom of the page, too. Can it be accomplished for individual pages or only for the entire document? If footnoting is required, it's important to be able to change bottom margins.

Can you request that the "pitch" (number of characters per inch) be changed for only a portion of a document? The same for the number of lines per inch. That nice feature will allow you to change the visual appearance of a page so correspondence will look less like typewritten copy.

Documents that are longer than a single page may require headings and footings. How varied would you like them? Some programs will handle only a single line, others two or three. At the same time, they may allow you to move the number position from the bottom of the page to the heading, or place them on another position in the line. Ideally, you should be able to turn off page numbering. Who wants a number 1 in the bottom center of a business letter?

Can you begin numbering pages with any digit and not have to begin at 1? Programs that have the capability of sectioning a large document into chapters and sections may also be able to cite references between pages.

12. File Handling

After you have created several files on a disk, it isn't always easy to recall what you named them. Is the directory available in a form you can read easily? Will it appear with the editing menu? Can it be called upon while you are in a file? If you don't want it to appear, can you turn it off so it doesn't take time loading?

A good program will permit you to move a block of copy from the file you are currently editing to another without leaving the current file. It will also let you bring other files into the current file being edited. This will be done with a "file insert," "file read," "library insert," or similarly named command.

Can you delete one file while you're in another file? It's sometimes necessary to delete a backup file from a disk when there's no more space to write, and save the new file.

Saving is an essential procedure as you work. Some programs can save copy automatically every 500 words or so as you work, although that can be disconcerting. But you should be able to save copy and not leave a file (essential if there are likely to be electrical overloads, storms, or other events interrupting the electricity). You should be prompted to save a file before you quit an edit session.

The programs should supply "housekeeping" chores for your file rather than sending you back to the system to copy, delete, rename, or merge individual files. Only a few provide the status, or space remaining, on a disk. Many will let you open a "nondocument file," that is, a file that does not have automatic word wrap, page breaks, and returns. It is often used by programmers. It is essential for entering lists that require merge functions and those that have to be sorted. It is important, too, for preparing messages for telecommunications.

13. Printing

Print directives are many and varied. Even though the software may offer it, not all printers will support all commands. Generally those you should look for are the ability to print underlining, boldface, subscript, and superscript. Proportional spacing and overtyping are not always so easy to find, but proportional spacing is nice when you want individual characters to occupy only the space they require so the final copy appears almost typeset. That's compared with nonproportional space where every letter occupies the same amount of space. Example: "i" and "m."

Will the print procedure allow the printer to pause and let you enter text at the terminal that can then be printed?

Can you stop printing and resume at the same place?

Can you request printing to be stopped so you can change a type element and achieve a different typeface using a daisy wheel or thimble printer?

How many copies can you request? The ability to request only a single print at a time can become tedious if you want multiple copies of a document. Want to type a letter and then change paper? Or insert an envelope? Then you should be able to request a pause between pages.

Can you begin to print on any page other than page 1? Also handy when you want to reprint only a single page in a long document. Without it, you would have to isolate the page in another file, then print it. Or to stop printing, you'd have to turn off the printer.

Can you include another file and piggyback it onto a first file and have the page numbering continue?

To save time, can you continue to use your computer to edit one file while another is being printed? That's sometimes called "spooling" or putting the file being printed in a buffer. It's like a "holding" place for the printed copy to wait until it's requested by the printer.

Can you elect to change an entire document typed in lower case to all upper case and vice versa? (Some systems commands can do this, but then formatting is not retained. Example is PIP[u] in CP/M.)

14. Enhancements

Many of the enhancements that might be in some programs are described in the chapters that follow. Merge, spelling, and document sectioning programs are showing up in more programs rather than as extras. This policy permits the software company to offer a better, more elegant package, and to minimize compatibility problems. It also provides a more valuable marketing strategy.

Other enhancements might be a math program that accompanies, or can be integrated with, the word processor so it can think it's also a calculator. Some programs will produce a word count of a document and an instant page count no matter where you are in the text.

Form letter generators usually accompany or integrate with mail merge programs (see Chapter 9).

15. Other

Every program comes with "defaults," which are the preset parameters. Can these defaults be readily changed by the user? "Readily" is a key word here! Some require that you reinstall the program; that can be such a chore it is easier to leave the defaults alone and suffer with those you don't like.

Does the program take full advantage of function keys, of arrow keys, and other individual features of a keyboard?

Can keys be redefined and assigned strings or a specific series of actions? These are referred to as "macros" (see Chapter 12).

As more programs compete in the market for your dollars, each company tries to outdo the other. Some may include a communications or "modem" program, another may offer a line drawing capability or a business graphics generator. Expect such additions to be in programs that require large memory capacities.

Add any others you may discover in the programs you find to evaluate for your specific needs or systems.

16. Keystroke Test Result

If you have implemented a keystroke comparison test, what feature did you select and what are the results for that specific program?

When you have questioned, defined, and tried to discover the meaning of every item and your answer to it, you're ready for a bachelor's degree in word processing analysis. You're also prepared for an intelligent decision about the word processing program to buy, or to evaluate the one you are using, and decide if a change is indicated.

At this writing there are reportedly more than 200 word processing programs for the MSDOS operating system alone. With additional programs for Apple, CP/M, TRS 80, Commodore, and other systems, it would be impossible to list them all. To help become familiar with different programs watch ads in magazines and list them based on:

Name of program _____
Manufacturer _____
Address _____
Phone _____
Operating system _____
Local distributor _____
List price _____
Discounted prices _____

Recommendations
Reviews in magazines _____
Friends, other users _____
Overall analysis/comments (based on needs in your Personal Program Profile). _____
_____
_____

You may have to write or telephone manufacturers for names of local distributors.

3. Checking Out Spelling Checkers

nly a few years ago, programs that would check spelling were rare, expensive, and in the luxury item class. Today the choice is mind-boggling, prices are lower, and many word processing programs include spell programs as a standard accessory.

Who is a candidate for a program that checks spelling by the miracle of computer electronics? Everyone who writes anything from a business letter to a book-length manuscript. People who admit their spelling and typing are far from perfect welcome these programs enthusiastically. But even those who believe they can out-Webster *Webster* will find that having the computer do the work saves time and eyestrain and increases efficiency. How? Why?

It takes time to read through a document on screen to find errors, place the cursor at the proper position, and correct the errors. What if you "think" you corrected a word and it is still misspelled?

A spelling program will never embarrass you; only you will know you have misspelled that word all your life. A spelling program will flag every typographical error and mismatched word in a very long manuscript in a fraction of the time it would take you to do it. An average read speed is about 1 minute for 2,000 words! Maybe 1½ minutes for 4,000 words. The time to correct takes longer; it depends on how the program is implemented and how quickly you are able to work through the flagged words.

That's only one benefit of an electronic proofreader. Knowing you don't have to clean up or retype pages when a single word is wrong encourages typing as fast as your fingers can keep up with your thoughts. If you mistype a word, you can fix it before it ever hits paper. Any number of errors, 150 to 200 in a 2,500-word (10-page) document, for example, may be repaired with an efficient spelling program in about 5 minutes

. . . probably less time than you would lose by typing more slowly. Using the program to do the tedious work is what computers are for!

The time saved will vary with different programs and people. But regardless of how good your spelling is, or how well you type, once you implement a good spelling checker, you may wonder how you ever worked without it.

Some programs do more than check spelling. Whether you need the other tools will depend upon the bulk and type of your word processing needs and how much you like to play with accessories. You can have such goodies as word count, word frequency, anagram, and homonym help.

If your correspondence consists of one-page business letters, you may not need a program that counts words for you, or reports on the frequency of different words used. If you're a writer with a 2,000-word assignment, it's nice to know when you're nearing or writing past the number of words needed. With word frequency lists, business people can remove redundancies from their presentations and students can improve their compositions.

SPELLERS WON'T TELL YOU WHAT YOU "MEANT" TO SAY

Generally, the good programs are clever . . . even brilliant and almost magical. But, be warned, they are not a complete substitute for knowing how to spell.

They may call a correct word "misspelled." Actually it is only mismatched. Any word that does not match a word in the dictionary is suspect. Obviously, the larger the dictionary, or the more specific a dictionary is for your needs, the better it will perform.

A program cannot guess what you "meant" to say when the error word you typed is also a word. For example, if you meant "and" but you typed "an," the speller won't toss it out as misspelled because both are legitimate words. Spell it "ane" and it will flag it. If you mean the word "sin" to be "sign," "sine," or "sing," it won't catch it as an error; sin is a word. Or if you type "generating" when you meant "generation," it won't tell you what you should have used.

IMPLEMENTATION CAUTIONS

Unfortunately, all spelling checkers are not created equal. Even if they all *appear* to offer the same features, an essential question that is hard to answer in a chart or comparative analysis is the speed of implementation. If the words are read quickly, but implementation is slow and awkward, the advantages of a speller are negated and may be discouraging. The same list could conceivably require 5 minutes to correct with one program and 30 minutes with another. They also vary greatly in size and type of dictionary, ability to detect words, limitations, accuracy, documentation, price, and support.

HOW DOES A SPELLING PROGRAM WORK?

When you request a spelling program to check a specific file it generally goes through two phases: the analysis phase, when it compares the file with the dictionary; and the interaction phase, the time when you decide how to handle the words and they are marked or corrected. It works as follows:

When you invoke the spell command and the file name to be checked, a control program tells the various parts of the system what to do. Your text is read and a unique word list is compiled and alphabetized. It is then compared word for word against those words in its dictionary. It usually tallies the number of words compared and then reports the number of "suspect" or "mismatched" words—those that do not match any in its dictionary.

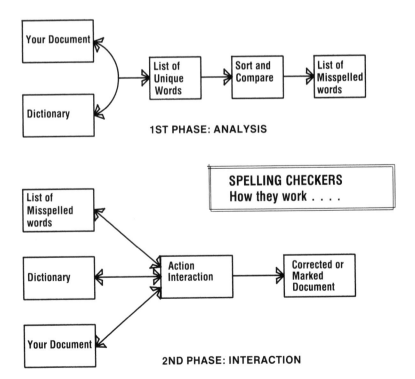

Next, the program goes into the interaction phase. It shows the error word, and you act upon it. There may be some back and forth action with the dictionary if the program gives look-up help, or the word appears in context. When all interaction is completed, either a mark is placed at the word in the file or the word is automatically corrected. In a program where the action occurs directly in the file, the word is corrected immediately; it becomes permanent when the file is saved.

ANALYZING THE CHARTS

The headings in the charts on pages 52–55 will provide insight into the available features. Not all programs have all features.

The list does not comprise all programs available. The information was compiled from a questionnaire. Companies who were solicited but did not respond were omitted. Inclusion or exclusion does not signify a recommendation against or a vote in favor of a specific program. Tastes and requirements differ.

The following explanations are numbered to coordinate with and explain the items in the chart.

1. Program and Requirements

Each program may require a different operating system, amount of memory, and disk space. Some will read files created by several word processors (stand alone) while others may work only with a host word processor. Be sure the disk is available in the 5¼- or 8-inch format you require. None of the companies responding offered them on the 3- or 3½-inch format at this time.

Version number and latest update are a consumer's protection. Updates appear so rapidly that is possible that your dealer still has an older version on his shelf. Be sure *you* know the latest version the company has distributed (it pays to make a long-distance phone call to the company to ask) before you accept a package. Your dealer may not know when updates appear.

Is it important for you to know in what source language the program is written? A user may wish to alter part of the program to his own specifications.

Stand alone programs, those that may run against several word processing programs, may require "installation" to work with a specific terminal and compatible software. If so, can you answer the installation questions? How will you know? Read the instructions in the manual before you buy the program, ask the dealer, or phone the company. Some can require that you dig into the manuals of the hardware. Ads may suggest that the program "permits" the user to configure it to his needs but in the real world that may mean that installation is required.

The amount of RAM memory and how much disk storage capacity is required must be considered. Interaction and dictionaries need space. There must be space for the spelling program, the dictionary, a backup of your file, and an error word list. If you are using 5¼-inch disks with only a 200K or less capacity, you cannot keep a dictionary of more than about 45,000 words available along with the control programs. Small disk capacity will limit the ability of a spelling program to perform.

Ideally, one should be able to keep the word processing and spelling programs on one disk. It is helpful, too, to be able to access the spelling program through the word processor.

2. Dictionary Data

The more comprehensive the dictionary, the more words it can compare and detect and the fewer words will be mismatched. But larger dictionaries also require more time to run against a document: a dictionary with 20,000 words will take less time to run than one with 85,000 words. Any dictionary with less than 20,000 words is not very useful. It will tend to display too many "suspect" words for the user to deal with and be inefficient when a document has to be rechecked several times.

A program should allow the user to either add to an existing dictionary or to create a supplemental dictionary. That's essential if you use a vocabulary with scientific words, medical words, or legal terms. If you're a plant grower you might want to create a Latin word dictionary.

Adding to an existing dictionary can be a trap. What if you add a word and misspell it? Can you delete it? (Some programs won't let you delete an added word.) Maybe you need additional words for only a specific document. It makes more sense to create a dictionary for that purpose and then run your file against both dictionaries. You can delete the extra one when you no longer need it.

The composition of a dictionary will vary. A "literal" dictionary is one with every word and its derivatives. Each derivative is counted as a separate word. "Do," "doing," "doer," "does," "redoes" would each be an entry.

A "root" word dictionary stores only root words along with rules for forming derivatives. It then reads the file for both root words and derivatives. "Do" would be the root word and then the dictionary would match any existing derivative words by automatically checking to see if *ing, er, es, re-*, etc., would match. Therefore, a 45,000-word literal dictionary could, in reality, present fewer "different" word matches than one with root words.

If root word dictionaries have a larger effective vocabulary, wouldn't they be preferred? Not necessarily. They can be less accurate and could easily accept a word such as "dedo" because *de* is a prefix. There are always trade-offs.

The majority of stand alone programs offer different ways to view the word after it is read against the dictionary. You can deal with each error in turn and have it either "marked only" or actually corrected in the file. Or you can request that the error words be listed without interaction. That's handy for a near-final draft, or in a short document when a quick listing may reveal only one or two errors. You can return to the document, find each error with a global search and make the correction. This avoids wading through a document that may have many "mismatched" words, not errors, such as proper names, abbreviations, etc.

3. Correcting Procedures

An essential consideration with any spelling check program is how easy is it for the user to indicate what is to be done with the word? The more automatic and flexible the procedures are, the faster it will be. Most programs present menus, some have help available at different steps of the action. Too many menus can clutter and slow up the procedure. (They're fine at the beginning, but can you eliminate them later?)The more direct the program is for showing the wrong word, enabling you to correct it, the faster the procedure will be. And then, how is the correction applied to the word in the file?

1. *MARK* word or *AUTOMATICALLY* correct? Programs work in two ways:

   a. MARK designates a program that *marks* a mismatched word in the file, then the user must go through the file, find the mark and correct the word. A program that marks only a word is generally slower and more tedious because the user must go through the document and make the correction. Usually, the program will move the cursor from marked word to marked word or facilitate the find in some way.

   b. AUTO designates a program that displays the mismatched word, the user corrects it, then the incorrect word is *automatically* replaced in the file.

Some programs offer the option of marking a word that causes a sentence to change length. Only a few programs will automatically reformat the line or paragraph but the trend in new versions is toward this capability.

2. How short a word and how long a word will the program report?

Will it show a lone, mistyped "t" as an error? Will it balk at a word the length of supercalifragilistic and its correction? Is it conceivable that a hyphenated word group will appear that way to the program? Will it break up the hyphens and treat them as separate words or as one word?

3. What type of interaction must you follow to correct the word? There may be nuances too subtle to display in a comparison chart. There's no substitute for trying a program yourself. But here are some possibilities and what to watch for.

    a. Generally you type in the entire new word. Some programs permit you to change only a few letters, but this is often more time-consuming. Some will also reject a wrong new word, which is a nice feature.

    b. A numbered list of optional words that are likely substitutes appears and you enter only the number for the correctly spelled word. That word will then appear in the corrected file.

4. Does program learn a typo and its correction? When the same misspelling recurs, it asks if you wish to use the same correction again and automatically enters the right word. You can also request that the word be remembered permanently.

5. Can you go back one or more words if you want to change your mind? It's inconvenient when you can't.

6. View in context. Can you see the word as it appears in the sentence? In programs that proceed through the actual document, that's no problem. But in programs that present only the mismatched word list, being able to view that word in context is helpful. If a view in context feature exists, how many lines does it show? one? two? three?

7. Can you *look up* the spelling of a misspelled word? How easily? Does the program automatically place the correct word in line when you ask it to? Or do you have to type it in? How many word choices are you offered?

8. In what "case" is the error word presented? Many programs show the error word in all upper case regardless of how it appears in the text. When it replaces the word, in what case will it be changed? Will you still have to retype it if the case differs?

4. Tutorials and Documentation

1. Tutorial. What user help does the program provide? Is there a sample tutorial on disk? in the manual? or both? A test document provided for a sample sweep provides practice and confidence to tackle your own file. The estimated time for learning the program is given by the distributor.

2. What kind of documentation is provided? How thorough? Is there a table of contents? An index? A command summary? A reference card? Until recently most documentation seemed hastily prepared, typed and multiprinted, then stapled. A sense of "temporary" until all the bugs were out was implied because documentation could be easily reprinted, or just a single page changed inexpensively. A printed package has the aura of permanence and "finished" and may indicate that the program is beyond the bug infestation condition.

5. Performance

1. Words read per minute. It is impossible to determine a meaningful time range for the number of words read per minute and the degree of accuracy for one program against another. Why?

The same program, run on different systems with different types of disk drives and with different chips, will vary considerably. It will vary between floppy disks and hard disks and with the number of error words found. Comparing programs with one another is even more "iffy."

A program that reads a 2,000-word document against any size dictionary in a minute or so is in the acceptable range. One that requires 3 minutes to read the same document is unacceptable. The human element is even more difficult to determine. Who knows how long it will take any one person to interact with the program? The same 40 spelling errors corrected by different people will require different amounts of time. In some programs, the actual change of words in the file will occur *after* all error words are retyped. In other programs, the error word is replaced as you work through the document.

2. Accuracy. Almost all questionnaire respondents suggested their programs were 100 percent accurate or close to it. In actual use, that wasn't always the case, especially in programs that read root words; some tended to miss repeats of the same misspelled word; or they didn't read enough of a word when a prefix anticipated the wrong root. Literal dictionaries rated higher on accuracy, but the 100 percent claim may suggest overconfidence.

3. Does the program make an automatic backup of your original file? If something happened to the copy you're working on there should be an untouched file. (Space on disk must be allowed for the backup copy.)

6. Bonus Features

1. Word count. Most programs tally a word count but may not consider it a feature. Some include a separate word count program that can be run to yield an instant tally. That's helpful if you're a writer who is paid by the word—maybe not necessary for business letter writers.

2. Word frequency or unique word count. How many times is each word used? A good feature for people who are bent on polishing their copy and perfect for the English-journalism student. It is not so essential for the majority of business applications. The word list should be able to be printed, written to file, and viewed on screen.

3. Does the program support a color monitor? Many do and they're more fun to use than the black and white variety for short documents. Color doesn't make you a better speller or cause the program to run any faster or more accurately than a black and white rendition. Color monitors tend to be hard to read for serious word processing applications. Highlighting, and reverse video, are nice if your terminal supports them. The error word shows up in color, especially when viewed in context.

THE WORD Plus offers anagrams and homonyms, and word find features using a "?" for unknown letters, among the extras. Electric Webster also has a grammar checker that works with the speller (see Chapter 4). Word Proof includes a synonym finder discussed in Chapter 5.

7. Support

If you have questions, problems, a program that doesn't work, or trouble installing the program, where can you go for help? Some programs put a "bug report" at the end of the manual so you can send it in. But who wants to wait for an answer when you have a program you paid for and want to use *now?* Is telephone help available? What hours? It should all be clearly stated in a manual or in the company's advertising.

Update policy? When new versions appear (as inevitably as day follows night), how will you know? Will you, as a registered user, be notified? And what will the update cost? "D" in the chart indicates the update is available from a dealer, "X" from the company, and a fee is usually involved.

The final answer for any spelling program is how well you can interact with it and whether or not it serves your needs. Fortunately, stand alone programs are not expensive; if you become familiar with what you like and don't like in a program and discover one that's better, it's worth the change. Spelling checkers that are tied in with a word processing program pose a different problem. You're stuck with that speller. If you don't like it usually a stand alone program will not work. Therefore, buying a word processing program today may mean investigating the spelling program, too, before you commit yourself to the whole package.

The following data was provided by the software companies. Some, but not all, programs were tested. Inclusion does not imply endorsement.

POPULAR SPELLING PROGRAMS

The following menus are representative of different spelling programs.

Electric Webster

```
         misspelled

in this sentence a mispelled word is considered a no-no and a

     Add word to:              Other Options:
     U>pdate Dictionary        P>revious word
     S>PECIALS.CMP             N>ext word
     M>ark word                R>esume review.
     D>iscard word             L>ook up word
     C>orrect word             V>iew context

  -->mispelled      Corrected to> misspelled
```

The Word Plus

```
·      The text line is shown across the top as a single or double line of type with
one INCORT word double underlined.

     UNKNOWN WORD: incort

Word correction mode—Options

  C —Correct word, prompt will follow
  D —Dictionary help. Find a word in dictionary
  L —Learn word for Auxiliary dictionary
  A —Accept word for rest of session, don't learn
  I —Ignore word just this once
  Q —Quit: abort session. No changes saved!
  E —END : Exit and save changes so far

C, D, L, A, I, Q, E, (H for Help)?
```

Random House Proofreader

```
(Perfect Writer) Perfect Speller Selection Menu © 1982 Perfect Software, Inc.

Available options for the Spelling Checker are:

     A —Add all the words in the file to the dictionary
     B —Change the backup file extension name
     D —Use the dictionary specified instead of DICTNARY.SPL
     L —List the misspelled words on the terminal
     M —Mark words with the specified characters instead of
     N —Make no backup of the file being checked
     O —Send all the output from Perfect Speller to the specified file
     P —Use the specified prefix/suffix table
     G —Start checking the spelling now
     X —Return to the top level of the menu

ps
Your Pleasure: (A, B, D, L, M, N, O, P, G, X) —
```

Perfect Speller

COMPANIES AND PROGRAMS

The following are listed in the same order they appear on the chart.

☐ **Benchmark**
Metasoft Corp.
6509 W. Frye Rd. Ste. 12
Chandler, AZ 85224
(602) 961-0003

☐ **Electric Webster**
Cornucopia Software, Inc.
P.O. Box 6111
Albany, CA 94706
(415) 524-8098

☐ **Memorite III**
Vector Graphic, Inc.
500 N. Ventu Pk. Rd.
Thousand Oaks, CA 91320
(805) 499-5831

☐ **Microspell**
Lifeboat Assoc.
1651 Third Ave.
New York, NY 10023
(212) 860-0300

☐ **Multimate**
Softword Systems, Inc.
52 Oakland Ave., North
East Hartford, CT 06108
(203) 522-2116

☐ **Perfect Speller**
Perfect Software
1001 Camelia
Berkeley, CA 94710
(415) 527-2626

☐ **Random House ProofReader**
Wang Electronic Publishing, Inc.
P.O. Box 327
Tijeras, NM 87059
(505) 281-3371

☐ **Spell**
The Software Toolworks
15223 Ventura Blvd. Ste. 1118
Sherman Oaks, CA 91403
(213) 986-4885

☐ **Spellright**
Structured Systems Group
5204 Claremont
Oakland, CA 94618
(415) 547-1567

☐ **Spellix**
Emerging Technology Consultants
2031 Broadway
Boulder, CO 80302
(303) 447-9495

☐ **SpellStar**
Micpro Intl Corp.
33 San Pablo Ave.
San Rafael, CA 94903
(415) 499-1200

☐ **Superspell**
Select Information Systems
919 Sir Francis Drake Blvd.
Kentfield, CA 94947
(415) 459-4003

☐ **Super Spellguard**
Sorcim
2310 Woody Ave.
San Jose, CA 95131
(408) 942-1727

☐ **THE WORD Plus**
Oasis Systems
2765 Reynard Way
San Diego, CA 92103
(619) 222-1153

(continued on page 56)

SPELLING CHECKERS CHARTS

CHART A

PROGRAM	REQUIREMENTS								
PROGRAM NAME	VERSION NUMBER	DATE	WORKS WITH DOS:*	SYSTEM SIZE K	DISK SIZE	SOURCE LANGUAGE	INSTALL REQUIRED	REQUIRES HOST W.P.	SIZE
CP/M—MSDOS—PCDOS									
Benchmark Spelling Ckr.	1.0E	7/80	1,2,3,4	3:64K 96K	5¼ & 8	Assmb'y	X	Yes	27K
Electric Webster	1983	1983	1,2,4	64K	5¼ & 8	Assmb'y	X		50KK
Memorite III	2.2	1982	1	64K	5¼	Mach	X-CP/M		30K
Microspell	4.4 & 5.1	1983	1,2	48K	5¼ & 8		X-CP/M		59K -
MultiMate Spell	3.2	1982	2	192K	5¼	Assmb'y		Yes	80K
Perfect Speller	1.1	1981	1,2	56K	5¼	"C"		Yes	50K
Random House ProofReader	1.1		1,2	64K	5¼		X		TO 80K
Spell	2.0		1,2,4	48-64K	5¼ & 8	"C"	X		50K
Spell Right	1.07	1982	1,2	56K	5¼ & 8		X	Yes	20K
Spellix	1.1	1983	2	128K	5¼	PASCAL			43K
Spellstar	3.3	1981	1,2	64K	5¼	Assmb'y	X	Yes	20K
Spellstar	4.0	1983	1	64K	5¼ & 8	"C"		Yes	55K
SuperSpell	3.0	1983	1,2	64K	5¼ & 8	"C" + Assmb		Yes	10K
Super Spellguard	2.1	1981	1,2	48K	5¼ & 8	Assmb'y			20K
THE WORD Plus	2.0	1981	1,2	64K	5¼ & 8	Assmb'y	X		45K
Word Proof	1.0	1983	2	96K	5¼	Assmb'y			125K -
APPLE AND OTHER									
Megaspell	1.0	1983	2,3	64K	5¼	Pascal		Yes	40K
Magic Words	1.01		3	48K	5¼	Assmb'y			14K
Sensible Speller	IV	1981	3	48K	5¼	Assmb'y	X		81K
Spell Handler	2.0	1983	3	48K	5¼	Assmb'y		Yes	90K
Spellproof	1.1	2a	5	18K	5¼	Assmb'y			21K
Spell Perfect	1.0	1982	3,6		5¼	Assmb'y			30K
The Dictionary	2.4	1981	3	48K	5¼	Assmb'y			28K
TRS 80 & OTHER									
Chextext		1981	4	48K	5¼	Assmb'y			20K
Corrector		1982	4	64K	5¼	Pascal	X		9 X 33K
Spellvue	1.0	1983	4,5	64K	5¼	"C"	X		32K

*Key to DOS column: 1 = CP/M; 2 = PCDOS and MSDOS; 3 = APPLE or APDOS; 4 = TRS-80; 5 = OASIS DOS; 6 = LJK DOS.

| DICTIONARY | | | CORRECTING PROCEDURES | | | | | | | | | |
R = ROOT / L = LITERAL	ADD-TO	EXTRA AVAIL.	HOW CORRECTED	ERR LETTER MINIMUM	WORD LIST	AUTO-INSERT	REPEAT LAST COR.	BACK STEP	HOW VIEWED	LOOKUP HELP	RETAIN CASE	HYPHENS AS 1 WORD
	X	By User	Mark	1		X			File	X	Yes	X
L	X		Auto	1	X	X	X	X	5 lines	X		X
R	X		Auto	2					File			
R		By User	Mark + Auto	1	X	X			1 line	X	Yes	X
R	X		Mark	1	X				File	X	Yes	
R	X	X	Mark + Auto	3		X	X	X	File		Yes	
L	X	X	Mark + Auto	2		X	X		File	X	Yes	X
	X		Mark + Auto	2					File			X
	X		Mark			X					Yes	X
L	X		Mark	2				X	File			
L			Mark						File		Yes	X
L			Auto			X	X	X	5 line/file		Yes	X
	X		Mark	1				X				
L	X	83K	Mark	2						X		X
L	X		Mark	2	X	X	X	X	1 line	X	Yes	X
R			Mark + Auto		X	X	X	X	File	X		
L	X		Auto	1		X	X		5 lines	X	Yes	
L	X		Mark + Auto	2		X		X	2 lines			X
	X	XX	Mark	1		X		X	File	X	Yes	X
			Mark	2				X				
L	X		Mark	1						X	Upper	X
(1)	X		Auto	3	X		X	X	4 lines	X	Yes	X
L	X		Mark	1			X	X	50 Charact	X	Yes	
L												
L												

CHART B

PROGRAM NAME	PRICE COST PROGRAM	M = MANUAL S = SCREEN	EST TIME REQUIRED	MANUAL BINDER †	PAGES	INDEX TBLE CONT	SUMMARY
CP/M—MSDOS—PCDOS							
Benchmark Spelling Ckr.	175.00	M	1 Day	A	21	I	X
Electric Webster	149.00	M	30 Min	B	64	TC	
Microspell	139.00	M S		A	58	I + TC	X
Memorite III	*450.00	M	4 Hrs	A	135	I	X
MultiMate Spell	*495.00	M S	1 Hr	A	5	TC	X
Perfect Speller	*450.00	M S		D	29	I	X
Random House ProofReader	50.00	M	5 Min	C	32	TC	X
Spell	49.95		20 Min	C	21	TC	
Spell Right	*495.00	M	5 Min	A	200(1)	I	X
Spellix	95.00	M S	20 Min	A	32	TC	X
SpellStar 3.3	250.00	M S	30 Min	A	19 +	I + TC	X
SpellStar 4.0	250.00	M S	10 Min	A	27 +	I + TC	X
SuperSpell	*495.00	S	90 Min	B	236(1)	I + TC	X
Super Spellguard	195.00	M	10 Min			I + TC	X
THE WORD Plus	150.00	M	15 Min	C	48	TC	X
Word Proof	* 60.00	M S		A	190	I + TC	
APPLE & OTHERS							
Megaspell	99.95	M S	5 Min	B	45	I + TC	X
Magic Words	69.95	M	30 Min	E	51	TC	
Sensible Speller	125.00	M	30 Min	A	102	I + TC	
Spell Handler	59.95		5 Min	A	5		
Spell Perfect	89.95	M S	1 Hr	A	75	I + TC	X
Spellproof		M S	1 Hr	A	106		
The Dictionary	99.95		1 Hr	A	39	TC	
TRS 80 & OTHER							
Chextext	59.95	M S	30 Min	F	12	TC	
Corrector	250.00	M	10 Min	A	79	TC	
Spellvue	195.00	M		A	56	I + TC	X

An asterisk next to the price reflects a combined word processor and spelling checker.

† Key to binder column: A = 3-ring; B = Plastic ring; C = stapled; D = perfect binding; E = spiral bound; F = plastic jacket.

REFERENCE CARD	WORDS PER MINUTE	% ACCURACY	WORD COUNT	UNIQUE WORDS	COLOR	REVERSE VIDEO	PHONE	MAIL	UPDATE
			X	X		X	X	X	X
	1200		X	X			X	X	X
						X	Dealer		
X	4K	90%	X			X	Dealer		
	150	100%	X			X	X	X	X
X	4K		X	X			X	X	X
	4K		X	X		X	X	X	X
		96%	X				X	X	X
X		95%	X	X	X		X	X	X
	3000	96%			X	X	X	X	D + $
X	51	95%	X			X	Dealer		Fee
X	2500	99%	X			X	Dealer		25.00
X	2000		X	X	X	X	X	X	X
	40K		X	X			X	X	D + $
	12K	100%	X	X			X	X	Cert. + $
				Thesaurus			X	X	
	2000	100%				X	X	X	Fee
	1600	98%				X	X	X	Fee
		100%	X	X		X	X	X	D + $
	60	100%	X	X			X	X	D + $
	30K	100%	X	X	X	X	X	X	X
	30K	100%	X	X			X	X	Fee
	2000	100%	X	X			X	X	D + $
	100	100%	X				X	X	D
	600		X	X		X	X	X	Fee
	1000	98%	X			X	X	X	Fee

☐ **Word Proof**
IBM
P.O. Box 1328
Boca Raton, FL 33432
(305) 998-2000

☐ **Megaspell**
Megahaus Corp.
5307 Oberlin
San Diego, CA 92121
(619) 450-1230

☐ **Magic Words**
Artsci, Inc.
5547 Satsuma Ave.
North Hollywood, CA 91001
(213) 985-5763

☐ **The Sensible Speller**
Sensible Software, Inc.
6619 Perham Dr.
West Bloomfield, MI 48033
(313) 399-8877

☐ **Spell Handler**
Silicon Valley Systems
1625 El Camino Real
Belmont, CA 94002
(415) 593-4344

☐ **Spell Perfect**
LJK Enterprises, Inc.
7852 Big Bend Blvd.
St. Louis, MO 63119
(314) 962-1855

☐ **Spellproof**
Quantum Information Systems, Inc.
145 N.W. 85th St. No. 103
Seattle, WA 98117
(206) 789-2888

☐ **The Dictionary**
Sierra On-Line, Inc.
Sierra On-Line Bldg.
Coarsegold, CA 93614
(209) 683-6858

☐ **Chextext**
Apparat, Inc.
4401 S. Tamarac Pkwy.
Denver, CO 80237
(303) 741-1778

☐ **Corrector**
Supersoft, Inc.
P.O. Box 1628
Champaign, IL 61820
(217) 359-2112

☐ **Spellvue**
Computer Printed Words
20219 Westridge Ct.
Castro Valley, CA 94546
(415) 537-9666

4. Your Silent Critic —Punctuation, Phrase, and Style Helpers

ou've cleaned up your document with a spelling program. You think it's letter perfect. Are you satisfied you've done the best you can?

Not if you proceed further with electronic tools. There are programs that can check punctuation, style, clichés, question incorrect word usage, and analyze your document with a grammatical word survey. People who are not trained in the nuances of professional composition may never have learned, or perhaps have forgotten, some of the no-no's taught in high school English classes. As children, many of us learned wrong speech patterns that are repeated in our writing (always blame it on your mother!).

Programs that can help you achieve word use perfection are Grammatik (Wang Electronic Publishing), "Punctuation" + Style (Oasis Systems) and Electric Webster (Cornucopia Software). Each should be used after spelling is corrected. But such a program takes time to use. If your documents need correcting, you can't afford not to take advantage of the programs.

The programs do have limitations. They are not the University of Chicago staff showing you every entry in the *Manual of Style.* They are not Webster pointing out the use of a wrong word in specific context. Nor are they Miss Manners, with an elocution lesson on the best way to deliver a thought. They won't tell you when a subject and verb disagree.

GENERAL PROCEDURE

Generally, you use the programs as follows:

1. Create a document with your word processing program.
2. Correct the spelling errors.
3. Analyze the document with the punctuation and/or phrase checker.
4. Revise the document with the word processing program.
5. Repeat the document analysis after further editing until you are satisfied with the corrections.

WHAT KIND OF PUNCTUATION ERRORS WILL IT CATCH?

It's probable that documents do not have consistent spacing between a period and the next sentence. Sometimes the shift key is held too long and the first two letters of a word are capitalized. It's easy to forget to delete a word and "two two" of them may appear. What if the period is on the wrong side of a parenthesis mark? Or if there is only one parenthesis or quotation mark when they should be paired?

The programs will flag all of these errors and more. You can ignore any of the suggested corrections, of course. Nothing is etched in stone.

Lest you believe the program will heal all your punctuation problems, let it be known that it catches only mechanical errors, not intellectual choices. It won't know where commas are improperly placed, or tell you where they should be used.

WHAT ARE CONSIDERED MISUSED PHRASES?

Often people unwittingly use phrases that are clichés, redundant, awkward, pompous, too vague, or outright erroneous. (Maybe you never realized there is no such word as "reoccur," it's recur.) It's possible, too, that your vocabulary could have a little more pizzazz poured into it. You can become aware of favorite words or phrases you use too often and these habits can be changed. Any phrases you know you overuse, or sentence structures you may butcher, can be added to a program's list. It can be your silent literary critic.

There are long-range benefits. After you become aware of problem phrases a program flags, you'll avoid them as you write. You will become your own editor in self-defense. You'll want to "beat" the program at its own game—and reduce the time required to run through a document. To help along these lines, the manual for "Punctuation" + Style presents the list of no-no phrases with suggested corrections in the manual. Grammatik and Electric Webster lists can be read on screen through your word processor and printed out for reference.

HOW THE PROGRAMS READ A FILE

The programs proceed similarly to a spelling checker but with a significant difference. A speller compares each word in a document against a dictionary of individual words and any word not matched is suspect.

A punctuation and phrase program's "dictionaries" consist of specific punctuation misuses or groups of words that form phrases. A "phrase" is composed of commonly misused word combinations. The categories will become clear as you read what each program considers "misuses" and compare them in the chart on page 69. When the program reads your file it finds phrases that match its phrase dictionary and points them out to you. You can interact in several ways with the suggestion, depending on the program. These might be MARK it, PRINT it, IGNORE it. Only Electric Webster lets you correct as you go.

Important questions to ask about each of these programs are:

How does it perform its analysis and point out the culprits?
What are your options?
How do you find the corrections in the document?
How do you correct the errors?
What additional helpful information does it provide?
Can you customize the "dictionaries"?
How easily can the procedures be changed from the default?

Unfortunately the one feature all the programs lack is the ability to reverse, or go back to a previous display if you change your mind.

GRAMMATIK

Grammatik was the first program of this type on the market, introduced in 1981 with a spelling program. That spelling program has been revised and is the Random House ProofReader. Grammatik is now an independent program that consists of five tools:

1. GMK—(Grammatik) is the main document analysis program. It checks the document for punctuation errors and reads the phrase dictionary during the same sweep through the file.
2. PHRASES.GMK is the main phrase dictionary and includes more than 500 phrases and words used to analyze the document; it has error categories and alternative suggestions for misused words.
3. SEXIST.GMK is a dictionary of about 100 commonly used "sexist terms" that flags use of words such as "chairman," "mailman."

   Both dictionaries may be "customized" by adding or deleting phrases through your word processing program using the same format as those already in the file.

4. PROFILE is a separate tool which lists the number of times each word is used in a file. It is similar to the tool "Word Frequency," offered with THE WORD Plus spelling checker (Chapter 3). A comparison of how these words are presented in the two programs is shown on pages 64–65.
5. SORTDICT may be used to sort phrase dictionaries and other text files.

How Grammatik Proceeds

When GMK is invoked the following menu appears that permits the user to reset any of the defaults.

```
Aspen Software Grammatik ᵗᵐ CP/M V1.x
  (c) ( ) 1981 Aspen Software Company
Command, <> = optional /Meaning/ Current setting

    C< = file>                Read configuration file
    D< = file>                Read dictionary                   PHRASES.GMK
    E< = list>                Errors, or NO to exclude ABC.....XYZ
    F = Char                  Set format command char
    I = file                  Set file to check
    L< = file>                List errors on file
    O< = file>                Output with errors marked
    P OR NOP                  Print errors on printer           NOP
    S or NOS                  Show suggestions                  S
        or NOT Show errors on TTY screen T
        or NOW Wait when error displayed W
    //                        Done-begin checking
                              (Use Control-C to abort)


*****Enter any command: ——>
```

After the dictionary is selected, E< = list> includes 18 letters each with an accompanying selection keyed to the manual showing the types of punctuation and phrases the dictionary flags. You can request that only some of the errors be checked—perhaps you're not guilty of using all of them. Here's what they include:

A. Archaic use. Words that have fallen out of common usage.
B. Unbalanced pair of ( ) {} [] ". These are counted and reported at the end of the analysis phase.
C. Capitalization error. Grammatik checks for consistent capitalization. Words that begin with the single letter "I" must be capitalized. Other words must be either all lower case or all upper case, or have a capital letter only as the first letter of the word.

D. Double word or double punctuation. Has something like "the the" slipped into the text? Grammatik will catch it. It will check for double punctuation marks such as "??", "..", "--", "!!" and ";;".

E. Error—unspecified. Reserved for errors in a user dictionary.

G. Gender specific term—to note words in the SEXIST.GMK dictionary.

I. Informal usage. Such words as "ain't," "anyways," and suggestions for using the proper nonslang words "are not" and "anyway."

J. Jargon or technical terms the reader might wish to put into his own dictionaries and mark as jargon for a specific document.

K. Awkward usage will flag phrases such as "and/or" and recommend revision.

M. Commonly misused words. They may or may not be used incorrectly in the text but the program flags them should you need to recheck. These include words that are similar, as "eminent," "imminent," and "immanent."

O. Overworked or trite. Such phrases are usually considered clichés. An example might be "crack of dawn," "busy as a," "crying shame," and others. You can add more of your own.

P. Punctuation error. There are several errors that will be detected, including spaces missing after a punctuation mark, and punctuation outside of quotation marks when it belongs inside at the end of a sentence.

R. Redundant phrase—such as "absolutely essential," "adequate enough" are candidates for revision.

S. Spelling errors. Grammatik can detect some spelling errors such as "there fore" "with out" "can not" that would not be tagged suspect by a spelling checker because each separate part of the word is a word itself.

T. Trademark. Certain words such as Coca-Cola, Xerox, Kleenex are trademarks that should either be changed to generic words such as cola, photocopies, or tissues, or else capitalized.

U. Improper usage—words such as "must of" will be flagged for correction to "must have."

V. Vague adverbs such as "basically," "essentially," "fairly," and "quite" will be flagged for attention and a more precise word suggested.

W. Wordy phrase—probably the largest portion of the dictionary. It includes phrases such as "all of" or "a half of" or "a large number of" each with suggestions for revising to "all," "half of" or "many."

How You Interact with the Program

The comparison of text to dictionary is shown to you during the interaction phase. The document scrolls on screen. When a matching phrase is detected, the scrolling stops. The phrase is repeated at an arrow, its line number in the text is given, and a suggested change is offered. It all takes place at the bottom of your screen as:

> Your actual text will be scrolled here but when a suspect phrase is encountered, the text will stop rolling and in order to
>
> ————> in order to
> * At sentence 46—'W'—Wordy phrase
> * Suggestion: to
> * Press: RETURN to continue
> *   or   Q first to quit checking

By selecting options from the menu before the check begins, you can note the corrections on screen, print them out, or mark them in the text. The original version will not be marked. An automatic backup copy is made (be sure there's enough room on the disk). The backup copy will be marked with an asterisk * (or other symbol you may select) in front of the word and an "x with a number" that matches the error category. To correct the phrase or punctuation, you return to the file with your word processor and use a global search to locate the markers. Suggestions for correction will not be shown, but if you request a print-out, the suggestion will be listed there.

Statistical Analysis of the Document

When the entire document has been checked, the program offers a fascinating statistical summary of the document. For example:

> Summary for FILENAME.TXT/ Problems detected: 26
>
> * Sentences: 204; words 2402
> avg sent len: 18.4 ; avg word len : 4.3
> # : 2 * imperatives: 3
>   sent (<12 wds) : 75 ; long sent (30 wds): 24
> longest 45 wds at #28; shortest 4 wds at #84
> to be's: 110 ; prepositions: 203
> User category totals:
> #3: 22 #4: 7
>
> ————————————————————————————
> Enter: Q or RETURN to exit
>   or   A to check another file: ___

In this analysis your silent critic is whispering information that may help your writing as much as any other aspect of the program.

```
straight paper path.  The hopper will hold 30 sheets at a time and

process them without operator attention.  Text can be sent via an

autodialer to a printer and private communication lines, to a word

processor, or to a host computer system.

          Courtesy, TOTEC CO., Ltd.
**** end of file ****
------------------------------------------------
Summary for I=B:CH110CR / Problems detected: 17

   # sent: 122 ; # words: 2035
   avg sent len: 16.9 ; avg word len: 4.7
   # questions: 11 ; # imperatives: 0
   short sent (< 14 wds): 49 ; long sent () 30 wds): 13
   longest 41 wds at sent # 102 ; shortest 0 wds at # 1
   to be's:.0 ; prepositions: 0
   User category totals:
       NONE
------------------------------------------------
Enter: E or just RETURN to exit
   or  A to check another file: _
                                            0:33:43
```

Grammatik's Document Analysis

The top line gives the file name and number of problems detected followed by:

First line: total number of sentences and words.

Second line: average sentence length and the average word length. (Writing manuals suggest that no sentence be longer than 26 words average.) If your document has an inordinate number of long sentences and exceeds this average, you may wish to revise the long sentences.

Third line: The number of interrogative sentences (?) and imperative sentences (!).

Fourth and fifth lines: line number in the document where the longest and shortest sentences and words appear.

Sixth line: totals of to-be's and prepositions that indicate measure of style. A high ratio of these to the total number of sentences indicates they've been overused.

Seventh line: User categories are established by the user and can be added to the PHRASE.GMK. Categories that might be selected by a user could be the number of times "that" or "which" were used. After using the program awhile a writer becomes attuned to his own style problems and can customize the program to his specific needs.

Profile

Profile is a separate tool that reports the number of times each word appears in a document; it is completely different from the statistical summary of Grammatik. It is run directly from the operating system or through the run feature of the word processor.

The list it compiles will be displayed on screen, in a new file, or on the printer (or all three). It's another chance to spot misspelled words, and to detect the extent of your vocabulary. The list appears with a number above each group of words. All words under *** 1 *** are those that appear one time in the document.

Aspen Software Grammatik Word Use Profile V1
Total number of different words: 104

********** 1 **********

addition	balanced	build	can	capitalization
caught	certain	check	comes	common
commonly	complete	consistent	contains	cp
dictionaries	discovered	document	each	electric
enough	errors	example	files	found

********** 2 **********

also	checker	checks	dictionary	ever
in	may	number	or	seldom
sexist	spelling	terms	will	word
works	your			

********** 3 **********

all	be	by	it	such
the	words			

********** 4 **********

as	for	grammatik	with

********** 7 **********

a	and	of

Comparison with Word Frequency in THE WORD Plus

This is an opportune place to compare the output of a similar tool offered in THE WORD Plus spelling checker titled WORDFREQ or "word frequency." The user can choose to have the words appear in the order of number of times each is used (column 1) or in alphabetical order (column 2). Both lists cannot be created simultaneously; these options are shown only to illustrate how the program works. To alphabetize the list, a "switch" $A for "alphabetical" is typed after the file name. (Switch options in THE WORD Plus compare to menu choices in Grammatik.)

As the analysis proceeds, the screen reports the total words, unique words, and number of words appearing once. The analysis is placed in a separate file with the same name as the original but with the extension of .FRQ as FILENAME.FRQ. It can then be brought on the screen or printed out as a word processing file.

Using WORDFREQ SAMPLE.TXT		Using WORDFREQ SAMPLE.TXT $A	
8	OF	7	A
7	A	1	ADDITION
7	AND	3	ALL
4	FOR	2	ALSO
4	AS	7	AND
4	WITH	4	AS
4	GRAMMATIK	1	BALANCED

"PUNCTUATION" + STYLE

"Punctuation" + Style is a companion program to THE WORD Plus spell checker from Oasis Systems. It was developed later than Grammatik and essentially performs the same tasks but in a different set of procedures. It offers a larger dictionary of problem phrases and therefore may take longer to use. There is a wide selection of procedure options. P + S will place the suggested correction in the text by default. When you return to the text the suggestions appear where they apply. The text must be revised, the marks and the suggestions deleted. The suggestion may be automatically inserted as an option. The mark and suggestion placement in the text are optional and can be overridden using a "switch."

The program is divided into two parts: PUNCTUATION uses the CLEANUP program to flag 24 kinds of punctuation errors. STYLE uses the PHRASE program to weed out poor phrase usage that the program's author considers clichés, awkward, erroneous, folksy, muddy, pompous, redundant, and wordy. It provides options for such phrases and lets you decide whether you want the phrases added to the text.

How Punctuation and Cleanup Work

PUNCTUATION assumes that your typed input conforms to standard style requirements for the typed document. When they don't, they are flagged. You run:

A>CLEANUP FILENAME.MSS

In a few seconds CLEANUP will display the first error with a small caret, used as a pointer, indicating the error position in the context of a short portion of the text. This information is displayed at the bottom of the screen with a menu of three choices. A culprit sentence would appear as:

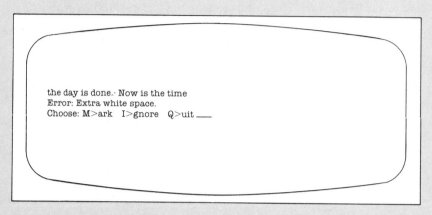

the day is done.· Now is the time
Error: Extra white space.
Choose: M>ark I>gnore Q>uit ___

"M" will mark a "@" in your document. "I" will ignore it, a "<CR>" will move to the next error, or "Q" will let you quit. When the document is completed, the number of errors will be noted. Corrections are made by returning to the document, finding the @ marks and correcting the document. (This @ mark can be changed if a specific program already uses that mark.) In the text, the information would be:

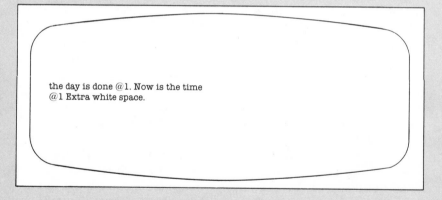

the day is done @1. Now is the time
@1 Extra white space.

The example shown is a minor correction. The program's virtue is in catching and alerting you to more serious mistakes. However, the suggestions clutter up your document and require time to correct and delete suggested "reasons." Errors might be:

Extra or missing punctuation.
Incorrectly spaced ellipses.
Incorrect abbreviations.
Missing capitalization at sentence beginning.
Incorrect capitalization such as "MIstake."
Unbalanced quotes, parentheses, etc., in a paragraph.

Unpaired underline and boldface commands.
Doubled words: "Now is the the time."
Incorrect form for numbers: $1,00.00."

Encountering such mistakes repeatedly can *teach* you those that you use incorrectly. In time, you'll catch them *before* you type them; that's where time and tedium will be reduced.

How Style-Phrase Program Works

PHRASE, the second portion of the program, searches for phrases that match entries in its phrase dictionary. A "phrase" can be a single word or several words in a certain order. The dictionary contains over 500 commonly misused phrases with suggestions for revising them:

In the following example the upper part of the screen shows the poorly used phrases to the left of the colon and the suggested better usage after it. The center part of the screen shows the full sentence with the culprit phrases in brackets. The bottom line has options for your action:

```
BEFORE IN THE PAST : BEFORE <OR> IN THE PAST
CONSENSUS OF OPINION : CONSENSUS
AS A GENERAL RULE : AS A RULE <OR> GENERALLY
MAXIMUM POSSIBLE : MAXIMUM

  [Before in the past] the [consensus of opinion] among
widget engineers was that widgets required at least one
hinge per load point, [as a general rule], to operate at [maximum possible]
efficiency.]

M>ark, I>gnore, P>rint, or S>uppress sentence? : ____
```

ELECTRIC WEBSTER

Electric Webster (Cornucopia Software) is both a full spelling and a grammar/punctuation checker in one package (although each can be purchased separately). The theory is that you should be able to progress directly from a spelling procedure to a grammar check procedure. It's a good theory and it works. It saves time. Electric Webster has features similar to those in "Punctuation" + Style and Grammatik, with several welcome garnishes of its own.

The main difference is that Electric Webster lets you type the correction *as you proceed* through the document, which is a definite plus. If a passive word, a verbose phrase, double word or punctuation are @@, you can type in the correction at that point. You can delete the phrase as you go or *accept* the suggestion. You will hear the disks whir as the change is made instantly so you need not return to your document, locate the offending phrase and then correct it.

Electric Webster offers phrase handling options as in the previous programs described; MARK the phrase in the document, IGNORE the suggestion, ACCEPT the suggestions, and so forth. The suspect phrase is followed by a series of ??? and the action choices are given in the menu that appears on screen as:

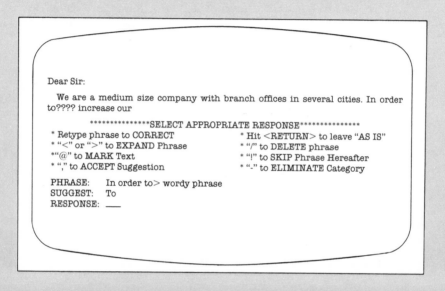

The defaults can be altered, including your decision about what length sentence is "too long." (Grammatik gives the sentence length average, line, and number of words in the longest sentence.) When the analysis is complete, a grammatical data survey is provided.

Electric Webster's manual does not reveal the total number of phrases checked but an in-use comparison appears to place it between the others. It seems more comprehensive than Grammatik and less than "Punctuation" + Style. But all programs can have phrases added and deleted.

COMPARISON CHART OF PROGRAM FEATURES

	GRAMMATIK	"PUNCTUATION" + STYLE	ELECTRIC WEBSTER
PUNCTUATION ERRORS			
Mixed U & L case	yes	yes	yes
Missing capitals	yes	yes	yes
Punc/quote wrong	yes	yes	yes
Missing end of sent.	yes	yes	yes
punc. or extra space	yes	yes	yes
Too much punctuation	yes	yes	yes
Isolated punctuation	yes	yes	yes
Unbalanced toggles	no	yes	no
Unbalanced quotes, brackets	yes	yes	yes
Numeric errors	no	yes	yes
Missing white space	yes	yes	yes
Word repeated	yes	yes	yes
Abbrev. expected	yes	yes	yes
Errors with dashes	yes	yes	yes
Unpaired underline/	no	yes	no
boldface (WordStar)	no	yes	no
Total types errors checked	15	24	22
Phrases Checked			
Archaic	yes	no	yes
Awkward	yes	yes	yes
Clichés	yes	yes	yes
Erroneous/misused	yes	yes	yes
Folksy	no	yes	yes
Gender	yes	no	no
Informal	yes	no	yes
Muddy	no	yes	yes
Pompous	no	yes	yes
Redundant	no	no	yes
Spelling (limited)	yes	no	yes
Trademark	yes	no	no
Trite	yes	no	yes
Vague adverb	yes	no	yes
Wordy	yes	yes	yes
Total number	"Over 500"	520	n/a
User can add or delete	yes	yes	yes
Alternate Suggestions	yes	yes	yes
on screen	yes	yes	yes
in document file	no	yes	no
hard copy	yes	editing	yes
Use of Passive "To Be"	counted	marked	yes
Document Analysis			
Number of words	yes	in spell prog.	yes
Number of sentences	yes	no	yes
Sentence lengths	yes	no	yes
Number of imperative sents.	yes	no	no
Number of interrogative sents.	yes	no	no
User categories can be added	yes	no	no
Word frequency	yes	in spell prog.	no
Manual	Fair	Fair	Fair
SUPPORT SYSTEMS	CP/M:MSDOS	CP/M:MSDOS	CP/M:MSDOS TRSDOS, APPLE
Price	$75	$125	$200 incl. Speller

COMPANIES AND PROGRAMS

☐ **Grammatik**
Wang Electronic Publishing, Inc.
Box 339
Tijeras, NM 87059
(505) 281-1634
PRICE $75

☐ **Electric Webster**
Cornucopia Software
1625 Beverly Place
Berkeley, CA 94707
(415) 524-8908
PRICE $200, including speller

☐ **"Punctuation" + Style**
Oasis Systems
2765 Reynard Way
San Diego, CA 92103
(619) 291-9489
PRICE $125

Similar programs may appear for other systems and by other software companies. As you see them advertised in catalogs and magazine ads, list those that will work with your equipment and investigate their features.

5. Finding Synonyms Electronically— Using a Thesaurus

The Random House Electronic Thesaurus was the first of its type on the market. Originally it was designed to work with WordStar and PeachText which were the most popular programs on the market. Since then versions have been written that are compatible with 16-bit systems using PCDOS and MSDOS operating systems. SYNONYM FINDER is a more recent offering that works similarly to the Random House program but with some enhancements.

IBM has a text editor, Word Proof, which includes a thesaurus and a spell checker. (See page 83.) The program can be used with only a few word processing programs: Volkswriter, Easy Writer II, The FinalWord. Other companies have similar programs on the drawing board. The following discussion will provide a basis for comparison and evaluation when such programs do become available. Ultimately, whether you have a choice will depend on the operating system and the word processing program you use.

The concept is a marvelous addition to the electronic library of any wordsmith who cares about writing well. It can be especially effective when coupled with a program that detects word frequency (see Grammatik's Profile and THE WORD Plus Word Frequency in Chapter 4). With these tools you may discover that you unintentionally overuse a certain word or words. Assume one word appears twelve times in one document.

How does the Thesaurus help? It could supply six, eight, or more synonyms with which you might replace some of the occurrences of the overused word.

A thesaurus has the potential to spark up writing tremendously. It could conceivably escalate everyone's communication ability from ordinary to extraordinary if the changes were employed in spoken communication, too. A wider vocabulary could infuse a dull speech with exciting words.

The Random House Electronic Thesaurus will offer up to 60,000 synonyms for 5,000 most used and overused words in English. A printed book of synonyms offers more, but the electronic application of the synonym finder might be more readily used when it's coordinated with your word processing. It works on your computer screen so you can look up a word and see the synonym list as you create a document. It will substitute a word you select immediately and insert it automatically into the text. Random House and SYNONYM FINDER temporarily replace the bottom portion of the screen with commands and list the synonyms across the top. Word Proof creates windows on the screen.

Documentation for these programs is minimal (not to be misconstrued as incomplete) because they do not require any more; they are that easy to use.

When you install the Random House Electronic Thesaurus, for example, an additional WordStar file is generated titled WST.COM. (That title is suggested by the Install program but you can give it any identity you like.) Or you can overwrite the original WS.COM file and then the Thesaurus will always be available. If you keep both, assuming you have enough space on disk, you have the option of using one or the other.

HOW THE RANDOM HOUSE ELECTRONIC THESAURUS IS USED

To use the Thesaurus your text may have to be on one disk with the installed Thesaurus on another. With ample space, or a hard disk, they could all be on one drive.

Use a copy of your word processor with Thesaurus installed (WST in WordStar) and call up the text file to be edited. When you find a word you may wish to change, place your cursor on the first letter of that word. Hit the escape key twice.

What happens? Your text drops to the lower portion of the screen, the word appears at the top of the screen followed by a list of synonyms tagged with the appropriate part of speech: adjective, noun, verb, etc. User directives appear across the middle of the screen. To select one of the listed words, hit the spacebar and the cursor will jump word by word across the list. When the cursor is on the desired word, hit the escape

key once and *voilà!* the new word will replace the old in your text. Hit
return and continue editing.

Here is how a portion of text would be handled on screen:

> If I were typing this document and I wished to find a word that was more
> exciting than some I used, I would be thrilled if I had an electronic thesaurus. If I
> were creating a thesaurus myself, I wouldn't have thought of making it as clever,
> simple and wonderful as did the author of this program. It is really ingenious.

Here's what would happen if the cursor was on the word "wonderful" in the copy and a synonym was requested. Hit the escape key twice.
In milliseconds, that copy would drop to the center of the screen and the
screen's top half would be temporarily replaced. The entire screen would
now appear as:

> wonderful—(adj.) marvelous, remarkable, awesome, miraculous, prodigious, astonishing,
> phenomenal, curious, strange, odd.
>
> <ESC> to change | <SPACEBAR> TO MOVE WORD RIGHT | (CTRL-W>   TO SCROLL UP |
> |<RETURN> TO EXIT | <BACKSPACE> TO MOVE WORD LEFT | <CTRL-Z> TO SCROLL DOWN |
> ═══════════════════════ The Random House Electronic Thesaurus ═══════════════════
>
> If I were typing this document and I wished to find a word that was more exciting than some I
> used, I would be thrilled if I had an electronic thesaurus. If I were creating a thesaurus myself,
> I wouldn't have thought of making it as clever, simple and wonderful as did the author of this
> program. It is really ingenious.

The cursor automatically is placed on the first letter of the first word
of the word list. The questionable word is highlighted (if the screen is
capable of it). You can move the cursor back and forth over the words
using the spacebar and back space. Once you decide on the synonym
you like, place the cursor on it, hit escape. The new synonym is instantly

substituted for the original word in the text. If you had selected "awesome" the screen would appear as:

---

wonderful—(adj.) marvelous, remarkable, awesome, miraculous, prodigious, astonishing, phenomenal, curious, strange, odd.

|<ESC> TO CHANGE | <SPACEBAR> TO MOVE WORD RIGHT |(CTRL-W> TO SCROLL UP |
|<RETURN> TO EXIT | <BACKSPACE> TO MOVE WORD LEFT | <CTRL-Z> TO SCROLL DOWN |

========================   The Random House Electronic Thesaurus   ========================

If I were typing this document and I wished to find a word that was more exciting than some I used, I would be thrilled if I had an electronic thesaurus. If I were creating a thesaurus myself, I wouldn't have thought of making it as clever, simple and awesome as did the author of this program. It is really ingenious.

It would be necessary to reformat the line when the word length differs.

The program also retains the case of a word. If the original word was all caps, the replacement word will be all caps.

What if the word is not listed? The Thesaurus looks for root words. It will automatically display words that are closest alphabetically to the word you want. A list of those words appears with the cursor positioned on the root word or the word alphabetically closest to the one in question.

Suppose you want a synonym for the word "used" in a line of copy. When you place the cursor on the word and hit escape twice, the screen will display:

---

used   IS NOT LISTED.   THESE WORDS ARE ALPHABETICALLY CLOSEST:

upper, uppermost, upright, uprising, uproar, upset, urbane, urge, urgent, use, useful, useless, user, usual, usually, utilize, utter, vacant, vacation, vacillate, vagabond, vibrant, vague, vain, vainglory, valiant, valid, validate.

|<ESC> TO CHANGE | <SPACEBAR> TO MOVE WORD RIGHT | (CTRL-W> TO SCROLL UP |
|<RETURN> TO EXIT | <BACKSPACE>TO MOVE WORD LEFT | <CTRL-Z> TO SCROLL DOWN |

========================   The Random House Electronic Thesaurus   ========================

Electronic programs are used frequently by smart computer operators to help them move beyond basic word processing programs.

With the cursor on the word "useful" in the list hit the escape key once. Next you will be offered all listed synonyms for "use," the root word. These will be arranged to show you which is a verb and which is a noun. The screen will now list:

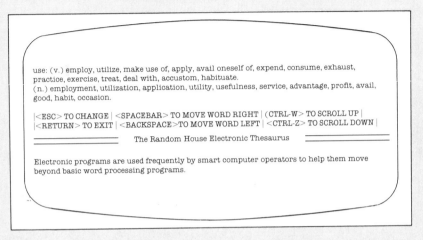

use: (v.) employ, utilize, make use of, apply, avail oneself of, expend, consume, exhaust, practice, exercise, treat, deal with, accustom, habituate.
(n.) employment, utilization, application, utility, usefulness, service, advantage, profit, avail, good, habit, occasion.

|<ESC> TO CHANGE | <SPACEBAR> TO MOVE WORD RIGHT | (CTRL-W> TO SCROLL UP |
|<RETURN> TO EXIT | <BACKSPACE>TO MOVE WORD LEFT | <CTRL-Z> TO SCROLL DOWN |
The Random House Electronic Thesaurus

Electronic programs are used frequently by smart computer operators to help them move beyond basic word processing programs.

To substitute "employ," press escape. Then add "ed" in the text for the proper tense.

What if you are happy with the word you have and do not wish to replace it? Hit return and the Thesaurus alternatives will disappear from the screen. The text will be fully redisplayed until the next time you question a word.

Thesaurus can also be implemented directly from the operating system to look up words "dictionary fashion" without replacing them in your text. You might do this if you're editing hard copy and want to determine if a synonym exists for a specific word. It may be faster than looking in a book. Call up a file named: RHT (Random House Thesaurus) directly from the A> prompt in the A drive. Press the return key and the menu of choices will appear. To display the synonyms for a word, type the word and press return. Move the cursor forward and back with a PLUS SIGN (+), a DASH (-) or a CONTROL J or a CONTROL K. To display the synonyms for another word in the list type an EQUAL SIGN (=). Type a QUESTION MARK (?) to redisplay the menu choice. A SLASH (/) will return you to the operating system. Any time you wish to test the Thesaurus to be sure it is performing properly type an EXCLAMATION MARK (!)

Options and More Features

Different-size versions are available: The 240K version offers 60,000 synonyms; an abridged 80K version offers about 20,000 synonyms. Which you use will depend on the disk capacity of your system. WordStar with Thesaurus.COM file installed requires about 90K of disk space plus the dictionary. A disk with less than 200K space would be difficult to use.

The program allows you to check the spelling of confusing words, too, such as principle and principal, insure and ensure.

You cannot add words and synonyms to the dictionary. The Random House Electronic Thesaurus is not meant to supplant a dictionary program; it is not designed to catch typos and misspellings. However, if you do have a misspelled word, which is actually a nonexistent word, the closest match will be found and that may be your clue that an error exists.

There's a side benefit, too. Anyone who is unsure of parts of speech and grammar usage will be exposed to which words are nouns, verbs, adverbs, pronouns, prepositions, and conjunctions. Such words are tagged, as illustrated in the examples, in the on-screen presentations. Some words will also be tagged as (informal) to indicate a popular usage that varies from the precise meaning of the entry words, or (slang) to designate a more extreme variance than informal and considered common usage but idiomatic or impolite. (Plural) is displayed when the plural form of an entry has a different meaning from the singular word.

Word puzzle buffs and word freaks who like to play word games could discover that Thesaurus is the best entertainment available on the terminal. Using it creatively could evolve an educational word game for youngsters, too. It's quick, convenient, reliable. It's a great tool.

Thesaurus requires CP/M or an equivalent such as TURBODOS, PCDOS, or MSDOS compatibility, and may be used with compatible MP/M systems and Apple computers with CP/M accessory cards. At least 57K RAM is recommended. The program will operate on hard disks.

SYNONYM FINDER, which has features similar to Thesaurus, contains an average of 7 synonyms for a dictionary that contains 8,500 words. It functions as a spell checker also. It requires 56KRAM and 160K disk space.

WORD PROOF

Word Proof is a text editor. A text editor is a less sophisticated form of a word processor more often used by programmers. It normally lacks the formatting and other advanced capabilities of a word processing program. Word Proof can be used in conjunction with compatible word processors such as EasyWriter II, Volkswriter, The FinalWord. It combines a 125,000-word spell checker and a thesaurus, for use only with MSDOS or PCDOS.

The synonym list is delivered on a separate disk. It places the list of synonyms in a "window" on screen. When the cursor is placed on a word and the F4 key is hit, Word Proof highlights the word, loads the list and puts up a "window" (the in-vogue word for a box) with the synonyms. It's smart enough to move the word up on the screen if it falls beneath the temporary window. Loading and displaying the window each time is terribly slow compared with the Random House program. It can take up to 12 seconds on a floppy disk system, but can be reduced to about 2 seconds if a disk emulator is used.

The more words displayed, the slower the loading. It does not display past tense and plurals and is easily fooled by irregular forms of common words. "Pay" has nearly forty synonyms offered, but there are none for "paid." You would have to type "pay," replace it with a word from the list, change it to past tense and then delete "paid."

Another problem? It will find synonyms for words with past tenses and plurals but the automatic replacement will be the regular form of the word. You have to change all suffixes.

When the entire screen is filled with words, you can page up or page down for the entire list.

Here's a simulation of how the screen would appear when the thesaurus program is used. The windows temporarily block out some of the text:

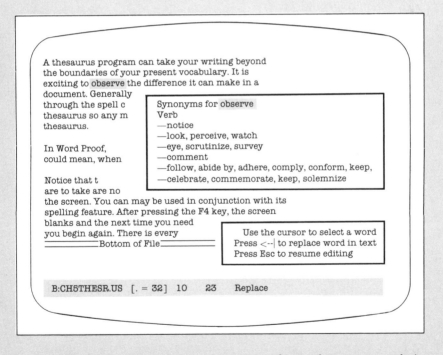

As other thesaurus programs appear on the market, compare their capabilities with those offered to help understand what they may be able to accomplish and how they are manipulated and integrated with a word processor. Watch for the number of references offered. A thesaurus with 2,000 or so synonyms might sound impressive in an advertisement, but it would be woefully inadequate in use.

COMPANIES AND PROGRAMS

□ Random House Electronic Thesaurus

Dictronics Publishing, Inc.
362 Fifth Ave.
New York, NY 10001
(212) 564-0746

and/or
Wang Electronic Publishing, Inc. (Formerly Aspen Software)
Box 339
Tijeras, NM 84709
(505) 821-1634
PRICE $150

□ Synonym Finder

Selfware
3545 Chain Bridge Rd. Ste. 3
Fairfax, VA 22030
(705) 352-2977
PRICE $199

□ Word Proof

IBM
P.O. Box 1328 C
Boca Raton, FL 33432
(305) 998-2000
PRICE $60

6. Referencing Programs: Footnotes, Bibliographies

nyone who must annotate a document with footnotes and endnotes will discover that most word processing programs lack this capability. Reflect for a moment on how footnotes and endnotes must be numbered when using a typewriter . . . each note is numbered in the text as you go, then proper spacing must be allowed at the bottom of that page. You must keep tabs on the numbers throughout a chapter, or a document. Should you decide to eliminate one of the notes, then all numbers following will need to be changed . . . and warrant a major retype job.

A word processor only, and no footnoting capability, will simplify the typewriter procedure somewhat. You can use a symbol to tag each call, type the note with a matching tag, then place that note in a separate file. When the document is completed you can perform a global search for each tag, call the matching note back from its file and place it on the bottom of that page (providing your word processor shows page breaks). It's still time consuming. The saving feature is that the computer and printer can redo the document in a fraction of the time and effort required with traditional typing.

HOW ELECTRONIC FOOTNOTING WORKS

The implementation and results of electronic footnoting will heighten your appreciation of its ability compared with the hassle required with a conventional typewriter or a program without a footnote feature.

Footnote Position　　　　　　　　**End Note Position**

Generally, this is the scenario on the computer screen.

You type text normally. But at the position you decide a note call is needed (a note call is a numeral (1) or [1] or ¹) you do not type the number. You type only the note itself, usually sandwiched between a specific pair of commands. The program then automatically does some or all of the following when the document is printed, depending upon the individual program:

1. Pulls the note from the body of the text and places a citation number at that point.
2. Places the notes with the matching number at the bottom of the proper page on which the matching citation number appears.
3. Formats the number in the paragraph, and also formats the notes consecutively throughout the document.
4. If additions or deletions are made it renumbers text references and footnote numbers and automatically places them on the correct page.
5. Creates a list of the footnotes, if desired.
6. Offers the option of placing the notes at the end of the text as endnotes.

Perfect Writer and The FinalWord are early word processing programs with the capability of doing all of the above. Word II by Samna will place footnotes and gather them as endnotes but the procedure is slightly different from the others. In Word II when you hit the MARK and F keys for Footnote, a window appears and you type "fff" plus the note in the window. The FFF is later replaced by the proper numbers. Several recently introduced MSDOS compatible programs include footnote capability.

A separate program, FOOTNOTE, can be integrated with files created with WordStar or Select word processors that run on CP/M or MSDOS systems. The supplemental programs MagicBind and MagicPrint are also independent CP/M programs with footnote capabilities. (See list at end of chapter for compatible word processing program versions.) Footnoting is only one of several features these programs provide; their main function is for customized printing formats using the Diablo and NEC Spinwriter for hard copy output. (See listing at end of chapter and also Chapter 10.) As demands for these features increase, more programs will undoubtedly appear.

How do you know if a program contains footnoting capability? If "footnoting" is not listed as a "feature" chances are it doesn't exist. But not always. Consult the table of contents or the index of a manual for footnoting but *do not confuse* "Footing" or "Footers" with Footnoting. Footing or Footers refers to the ability to change the bottom margin of a page.

While the odds are 100 percent in favor of electronic footnoting compared to the typewriter, that doesn't mean it's effortless. Nor does it mean everything will happen exactly as you envision. There are limitations in some programs as to the number of characters or lines that the printer can accept at the bottom of a page (endnoting is easier). Some trial and error will be involved, then adjustments may be needed to lengthen bottom page margins.

The limitations differ in programs and can usually be handled with experience and a change in formatting. Generally if a footnote is too long for one page, the program will spill it over to the next page. Footnotes will always be printed in single spacing. And there may be a maximum number of footnotes allowed in one document.

For programs that gather footnotes into endnotes, the parameters will differ. There may be a limit to the number of notes and the number of characters that may be gathered.

HOW DO YOU KNOW WHAT YOU NEED?

If you are considering a footnote and endnote program, select one of your earlier finished footnoted papers. Evaluate the number of footnotes per page, the average length of the footnote in characters, and the total number of lines required.

Try to average footnote per page needs and evaluate your requirements against the limitations in the program. These are usually listed in the manual where the footnote feature is explained, or in the possible list of error messages. If the limitations are not clearly marked, you might want to try inputting a heavily noted section using the program. (That's going to take time because you may have to learn to use the program, too.) It's all part of the search.

The other option is to select a specific word processing program because it offers the capability. What if it doesn't completely perform to your needs? You may have to change your note system to perform within its parameters. That could mean shortening and revising footnoting systems or dividing a document into smaller sections, then chaining or merge printing the sections together as one (see Chapter 9 on merge printing).

FOOTNOTE

Here's a sample of how the program FOOTNOTE by Pro/Tem, Inc. performs. The program integrates with WordStar text files and is slightly more complex than those that are integrated with a specific word processing package. It allows you to place notes anywhere in the text that is convenient for you, then it pulls out these notes, numbers the call at that point in the text, places them where you want them, and numbers them as it goes.

You enter text as usual, but where you wish to have a note call (Example: note call[1]), you enter an @. Then you sandwich the note itself between an ^R (CONTROL R), two carriage returns, and a .pa to end a note or group of notes. This is a WordStar method for forcing a new page and FOOTNOTE uses it to end the list of footnotes.

When you complete the document, with all the necessary symbols and notes, you save the file. Then you must run the FOOTNOTE program against the document. What happens? FOOTNOTE numbers the notes consecutively and formats the file. It places the notes at the bottom of the appropriate page or, at the user's option, moves them out of the text to a separate endnote file. The original file is saved as a backup file. If you wish to change anything, return to the backup file, do the necessary editing, then reformat again so FOOTNOTE can alter the text or renumber footnotes when changes occur.

Here is how a typed example would appear on screen if the note is placed in the middle of a paragraph. It will vary slightly if it's at the end of the paragraph or an endnote.

Four score and seven years ago@, our fathers brought˘R <CR>

 @ "Fourscore and seven" is 87 years. <CR>
<CR>
.pa <CR>
 forth on this continent a new nation ---etc.

When you subject this information to FOOTNOTE and view the resulting backup file it will appear in a new file with its control codes as:

Four score and seven years ago˘E˘T1˘T our fathers brought forth ˘Y˘Y.

However, when you print the file on paper it will be formatted with the dividing line and the numbers superscripted as:

Four score and seven years ago[1] our fathers brought forth

---
[1] "Fourscore and seven" is 87 years.

FOOTNOTE's initial menu offers the following six choices:

1 or N   Number notes
2 or F   Format footnotes in text file
3 or R   Remove notes from text file to endnote file
4 or M   Merge endnotes into text file
5 or C   Change default
6 or X   Exit to operating system

It asks for the name of the file and then you relax as it quickly performs its tasks. A first run-through numbers the notes. A second run-through formats.

A file that has been finally formatted or merged is usually ready for printing without further editing. But if a change is made, there is one caution. In the example above, the ˆYˆY that appears indicates extra linefeeds placed in the copy by FOOTNOTE. Therefore, one must never add text between the ˆY's and the footnote rule line.

There are a few limitations. When footnotes are too long for the line limitations, the extra lines may be carried to another page. However, if a single footnote exceeds 200 lines (quite a bit) or the total lines of all footnotes called from one document exceed 255 lines, the program will print an error message.

FOOTNOTE makes a backup copy of the file it is formatting so there must be ample disk space; a formatted file is always longer than the original because additional space is required.

The manual provides a list of errors and error messages and sensibly flags some as those the beginner might incur. It explains how to discover and overcome them readily. An example text is provided on disk which, if printed as hard copy, can become the user's easy reference to text preparation for FOOTNOTE.

FOOTNOTING IN PERFECT WRITER AND IN THE FINALWORD

Perfect Writer and The FinalWord word processing programs establish footnotes in documents by placing them at the bottom of a page or at the end of the document as endnotes. Both programs follow the same procedures. The examples shown are derived from Perfect Writer. It offers choices of:

1. Footnotes placed at the BOTTOM of the page or at the end of the text in a FOOTNOTE FORMAT and two options for positioning the numbers. The number in the text may be placed above the line as [1] (superscript) or the number can be within the line in brackets as [1].
2. NUMBERED NOTES (not in footnote format) printed at the END of the document.

Placement of notes within the text is accomplished with fewer commands than those required in the program FOOTNOTE described above. Place the citation, or note, in the body of the text where the citation is to appear as:

@FOOT(the note must be sandwiched between parentheses).

Each program that integrates a FOOTNOTE feature works in essentially the same way with minor variations.

Perfect Writer places the necessary number at that position, pulls the citation out of the text, styles it, and places it at the bottom of the proper page. All citations within a file are consecutively numbered. Should you delete or add any, all will be automatically renumbered. Formatting an entire document is a separate step in these programs and the footnote is formatted at the same time.

By default, a footnote is placed at the BOTTOM of the page on which it is referenced. However, all footnotes may be gathered and printed together AT THE END in the same footnote style; the proper STYLE command must be set at the beginning of the file. A similar but slightly different command called only @NOTE(followed by the text placed in parentheses) places a note at the end of the document but not in footnote format; it's a straight text format. The programs offer several choices which are easier to use than to describe.

On screen the copy with a footnote will appear as:

Footnotes placed on screen, as in the next paragraph, will appear on paper at the bottom of the page separated by a short line of dashes as shown below.

A typical reference footnote would be entered as: @FOOT(Smith, Mary, "How Computers Will Affect Your Tensions," @U[Today's Psychology], 1984, @U[4] pp. 89,90.) @FOOT(Smith, Mary, "How Computers Will Affect Your Tensions," @U[Today's Psychology], 1984, @U[4] pp. 89,90.)

On the printed page the notes would appear as shown. The @ is the command to underline that text.

— — — —

3. Smith, Mary, "How Computers Will Affect Your Tensions," Today's Psychology, 1984, 4 pp. 89,90.

Notes Formatted as Text

Perfect Writer and The FinalWord also allow you to place numbered notes within the text, at the bottom, or at the end of a document in text format rather than in footnote format. Instead of the command @FOOT-NOTE, use @NOTE. The @NOTE command functions the same way and each note is numbered throughout. To tell the program where you want the note to appear, you use a STYLE command at the beginning of the document as @STYLE(notes in line) or @STYLE(notes endnote).

Limitations

There are limitations that can create problems and dilute the wonder of "noting" capability. By default, footnotes can only be a specified number of characters. If a note extends beyond the space length allowed for the page bottom margin, the note will be cut off and that portion will be lost in the printout only. In an individual file the space can be increased with a STYLE VALUE command at the beginning of the file.

Endspace can also pose a problem if there are more notes than the program can accommodate in the "endspace." The procedures appear formidable especially the first few times they are used. The complexities and the many choices are sometimes so overwhelming that new users shy away from using them. They do take time to work out.

Set and Reference—Another Device

Another referencing feature that exists in Perfect Writer and The FinalWord is called SET AND REFERENCE. This lets you place a reference to a comment on a page or pages elsewhere in the text. The non-electronic procedure is to leave a blank space and when you know the page on which the item appears, go back and write it in. With set and

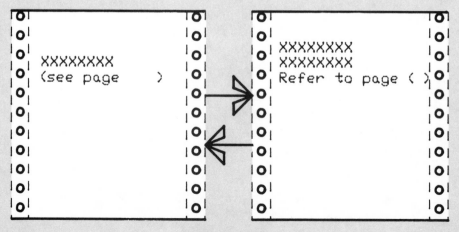

Set and Reference

reference, if you place the commands properly throughout a document, it will do it for you. However, the document must then be chain printed if the references appear in different chapters. If each chapter is paged and numbered individually, the feature will work only in that one chapter or in a single document.

You type the words to reference and place them using the @SET(the words to reference) and @REF(the words to reference). When the program encounters one or the other, it will place the proper page number where it belongs. During editing, if the page a reference is on changes, the program will re-reference that change automatically.

Here's how it appears on screen:

In this book there is a reference in an early chapter to a specific @STYLE command, footerspacing, to be used with ... etc. @SET(FOOTERSPACING = page)

Later, in another chapter the reference to the set page would be placed on screen as: (see page @ REF[FOOTERSPACING]).

On paper it would appear as:

In this book there is a reference in an early chapter to a specific @STYLE command, footerspacing, to be used with ... etc. (footerspacing page 10).

Later, in another chapter the reference to the set page would be placed on screen as: (see page 10 FOOTERSPACING)

BIBLIOGRAPHY

The program BIBLIOGRAPHY by Pro/Tem is designed to let you create a bibliography and then merge references to this bibliography in a text file.

The procedure involves constructing a bibliography for a given document as a Library File. Each entry in this library file would contain all books, or references, and conform to the given format such as:

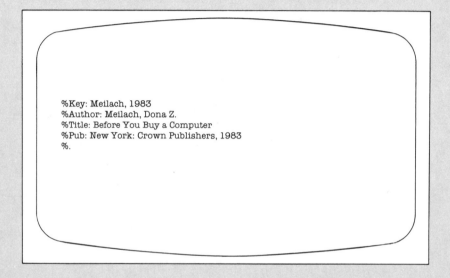

%Key: Meilach, 1983
%Author: Meilach, Dona Z.
%Title: Before You Buy a Computer
%Pub: New York: Crown Publishers, 1983
%.

Then, when you write the file, you reference the key words on screen as:

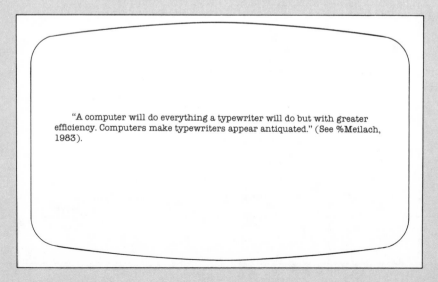

"A computer will do everything a typewriter will do but with greater efficiency. Computers make typewriters appear antiquated." (See %Meilach, 1983).

Before the document is printed, one of several formats may be requested. The entry can be concatenated; the keyname can be included or excluded; the entry can be numbered; the author's last name can be written in upper case; and annotations can be included or excluded.

Here are some samples of possible formats that BIBLIOGRAPHY can produce on paper:

Meilach, 1983
Meilach, Dona Z.
Before You Buy a Computer
New York: Crown Publishers, 1983

1. Meilach, Dona Z.
   Before You Buy a Computer
   New York: Crown Publishers, 1983

Meilach, Dona Z., Before You Buy a Computer
New York: Crown Publishers, 1983

BIBLIOGRAPHY can also leave the citation in the text as it is written and remove the %; it can replace the citation and number it to correspond to the order in which the entry appears in the bibliography; or it can replace the citation with the concatenated entry.

A Merge Bibliography command is included so that a user can construct a single alphabetized bibliography from several separate libraries.

BIBLIOGRAPHY is a unique program that can be used in conjunction with many word processors such as WordStar, Spellbinder, PeachText, and SuperWriter, and in most formats: CP/M 80, CP/M 86, and PCDOS and MSDOS. The CP/M 2.2 version will handle libraries with over 1,000 entries in a 64K system and more than 500 entries in a 48K system. The CP/M 86 and PCDOS versions require 64K minimum and will handle libraries of more than 1,000 entries in a 64K system.

The ability to automatically and electronically create footnote or endnote entries and generate a bibliography for a document are valuable adjuncts to word processing for attorneys, businessmen, journal writers, authors, teachers who prepare articles, and students who write term papers and theses.

COMPANIES AND PROGRAMS

□ BIBLIOGRAPHY
Pro/Tem Software, Inc.
Distributed by
Digital Marketing
2670 Cherry Lane
Walnut Creek, CA 94596
(415) 938-2880

CP/M, MSDOS, PCDOS, and
  compatible with most word
  processing programs.
Requires 48K or 64K in CP/M, 64K
  in MSDOS and PCDOS.
PRICE $125

□ FOOTNOTE
Pro/Tem Software, Inc.
Distributed by
Digital Marketing
2670 Cherry Lane
Walnut Creek, CA 94596
(415) 938-2880

CP/M, MSDOS, PCDOS, WordStar
  and Select word processing
  programs.
Requires 42K RAM.
PRICE $125

□ THE FINALWORD
Mark of the Unicorn
P.O. Box 423
Arlington, MA 02174
(617) 489-1387

CP/M, MSDOS, PCDOS. Included
  in The FinalWord word
  processing program.

□ MAGICBIND and MAGIC-PRINT
Computer EdiType Systems
509 Cathedral Pkwy.
New York, NY 10025
Distributed by Lifeboat Assoc.
1651 Third Ave.
New York, NY 10038
(212) 860-0300

CP/M, with 48K memory. Versions
  for use with Electric Pencil,
  Magic Wand, Mince, P/Mate,
  T/Maker, Word Master, WordStar.
Footnote capability is one portion
  of the overall program for
  detailed printing formats using
  Diablo and Nec Spinwriter
  printers. They also support the
  Baby Blue card for the IBM PC
  and the Softcard for the Apple.
PRICE $250 MagicBind, $195
  MagicPrint

□ PERFECT WRITER
Perfect Software
1001 Camelia St.
Berkeley, CA 94710

CP/M, MSDOS, PCDOS. Included
  in Perfect Writer word
  processing programs.
PRICE Varies for DOS. Often
  bundled with a computer system

□ WORD II and WORD III
Samna Corporation
2700 NE Expressway Ste. C-1200
Atlanta, GA 30345
(800) 244-2065
(404) 321-5006 (GA)

PCDOS, MSDOS. Footnoting
  included in the word processing
  program.
PRICE $450 for package WORD II
       $550 for package WORD III

7. Organizing Long Documents, Table of Contents, Index

ometimes what we wish could be done seems so impossible we bumble along the hard way without questioning the possibility of easier methods. The electronic organization of long documents offers a convenience and efficiency that are hard to imagine until you use the programs yourself on one of your own documents. You have to know the capability exists and how to take advantage of it.

How would it help your work to have a program that would integrate with your word processor to section and style a document into chapters, subheadings, sub-subheadings, paragraphs, appendices? Would it be helpful to have illustrations and tables keyed with the text and also generate a separate list at the end of the document? Would it confound the imagination to know that it could simultaneously create a comprehensive table of contents? And with a few additional procedures, it could generate an alphabetized index with each entry automatically referenced to the proper page?

Sound futuristic? Of course. Possible? Sure. Available now? Absolutely! The features in the programs described vary; they do not all perform their acts with equal facility and grace. But what they do accomplish could increase accuracy and save hours of work. Scan the chart on page 111 to learn what tasks are possible. Decide how you would want your documents sectioned. Then study which program offers features to accomplish your specific goals.

CREATING A TABLE OF CONTENTS

Generically, document sectioning programs are referred to as "indexing" programs. They also generate a table of contents which can serve as a subject guide to a document.

Imagine how a table of contents might be generated in days of yore when only typewriters and people coordinated it all. As each chapter was written, the writer would have to go through the printed copy and gather the headings, subheadings, paragraphs, etc. These would have to be individually typed, each adhering to the same levels and case as those used in the chapters. What if the writer wanted to delete or add a section? Or change a subhead to a paragraph entry? Scissors and paste or retyping would be the procedure. And if the sections were numbered, all subsequent sections would require renumbering.

With an electronic tool to do the job, you place a signal before every title for each heading level. The program reads that signal and styles the heading with a boldface, underline, or other established form. It can copy that heading to generate the table of contents complete with the page number on which it appears. Formatting a document averages 12 to 20 pages per minute with time variance caused by the number of entries marked.

When a heading entry requires editing, or deleting or adding, rerun the program and all the work will be done again in seconds—and without complaints. Page numbers will be updated automatically. Depending on the program, the table of contents may be placed at the end of the document or in a new file. You can use it as is, edit it, and print it. A table of contents from individual documents, or chapters, can be combined for an entire book.

A table of contents has wider implications than its role as a directory. It will show you, at a glance, if you have inadvertently made a subtitle into a title; you can tell, too, if all levels match in the use of capitals or capital and lower case letters. It helps you refine a document and establish a consistency so every document will appear as professional as possible.

Some programs offer more formatting flexibility than others. One may automatically place a relational number (1.1, 1.2, 1.3.1, 1.3.1.a, etc.) at each marked section of the document that you can't omit during printing even if you want to. If you *don't* want these numbers automatically generated in the document and the table of contents, you have to select a program that provides the option to omit them.

Before you invest in a program, observe printouts in computer documentation. (You probably have some in notebooks on your shelves that accompanied software.) Technical writers use indexing programs. Once you're aware of how they appear you'll be able to recognize differences. Observe those that have relational or regularly numbered level headings and how they are styled. Some have consistent spacing between headings and text and some do not. Compare a table of contents and an index in one manual with that in another. With less than 10 indexing programs available, you may be able to recognize which manual was developed with each program.

Creative Applications for Table of Contents Generators

Convenient document sectioning, generating a table of contents and an index are the prime, and promoted, purposes of the programs. With some improvisation they can be used to organize documents for other reasons and in different ways from those for which they were designed.

For example, you may hope to cover several thoughts in a document. You could tag these thoughts as you work. Run the document against an index program and each thought would be output as an entry in a "table of contents." Immediately you'll be able to determine if you have repeated yourself, omitted something, or placed a discussion in a wrong sequence. In essence, it is generating an instant outline with page numbers for each topic. You can quickly locate a concept and possibly improve a report, lecture, or other presentation before final printout.

A novelist and a screenwriter could keep track of each scene, each plot maneuver in a story.

An attorney and a real estate agent would know immediately which paragraph of a document has what clause.

An executive preparing a speech could tag each section as he goes, then have a quick summary of the subject using a generated table of contents for a review. This same summary, perhaps with slight editing and reformatting, could be used as the basis of a slide presentation. The slides could be created with a necessary graphics program, then photocopied with a 35mm camera from the screen. (There are companies that provide this service, too.)

A slide with titles for a speech can be photographed from the screen or produced from the text provided on a disk by a company that performs this service.

An author/illustrator could mark sections where illustrations would be added. They could be keyed into the document using number and page references generated by the indexing programs along with a separate list of the captions.

Anyone who has to leave a written document for any length of time, and return to it weeks or months later, will have a ready synopsis for review.

INDEXING

Indexing requires that you place a command before the words, or before and after a string of words, to be indexed. These must be added on each page that an entry appears. The program does the rest; it picks out the word, and an entry level you've designated. It sorts and alphabetizes the words and assigns the proper page number to them. In seconds! If you've ever indexed a project you'll appreciate this time-saver.

Each program requires a slightly different set of procedures. All will generate similar, but individualized, output. One or another, or perhaps two, can be a valuable addition to your software library if they fulfill your wish list and can be implemented quickly.

How an Index Happens

How readily can an alphabetized, page-numbered index be generated? Is it possible to overcome the tedium of indexing a book-size manuscript and banishing forever the mountain of 3 x 5 index cards?

Generating a subject index electronically for a short document is easy. Large text files are not as labor-free as one might fantasize. But once you learn to implement the programs the result could be a more thorough and accurate index than one generated using 3 x 5 cards and plowing through a document page by page.

Indexing requires time, practice, and motivation. Many more directives must be placed for an index than for a table of contents. And it is still *you* who must decide which words are to be indexed and how. The computer takes some tedium out of it; you still have to put the brain power into it.

When a document is completed you mark each entry to be indexed in the file. (Placing the marks can be tedious but shortcuts can be devised.) The entry can be one word or several words, depending on a specific program's limitations. The program will read these marked words into a new index file, alphabetize the entries, and arrange them in levels according to the directives given. Some programs generate only one level of indexing, others will generate two or three.

When is indexing effective and not effective? It is recommended when the final copy will be a result of the document formatted by the word processor.

It is not practical when a document will be typeset from the typed manuscript. Why? Typesetting generally results in different page numbering from the raw manuscript. The user would have to copy the original and reformat the pages to reflect exactly the pages of the typeset document. Then he would mark the index entries to match the typeset page numbering. In some cases, it may be as time effective to use the tried and true 3 x 5 index cards.

Possible Problems

To index a document, every occurrence of a word and subject on each page must be detected and either retyped or sandwiched between symbols. Variations of an entry would have to be added also. John Doe would have to be indexed as "Doe, John" and require retyping in the file.

Programs offer no way to check whether all occurrences of an entry have been found.

Always back up a copy of a document before you proceed and use the copy for the index. After a file is marked and keyed in, it's almost impossible to eliminate the commands. Some programs actually drop the marked string out of the file during formatting and the indexed file cannot be used again for printing.

DOCUMENTATION

All manuals are reasonably good and each provides a sample document on screen. The procedures become clearer as you study the sample text, run the program, and observe the results. Potential errors are clearly defined. No installation is required.

Print the sample document through the DOS capability of your system. It's easier to follow and refer to the command placement from a hard copy. Print the generated formatted file (usually it will have another extension name such as FILENAME.IDX) through the word processor. Referencing the command and the result will help to understand the procedures more quickly. Instructions for using the program may also appear in a file named READ.ME or FILENAME.DOC. (DOC stands for documentation.)

THE PROGRAMS EXAMINED

Reviews of five "index generating" programs will help you make a decision. DocuMate/Plus, WordIndex (both distributed by Lifeboat Associates), StarIndex (MicroPro International Corp.), INDEX Generator, written by Tom Jennings (the program is in the public domain), and Perfect Writer (Perfect Software). Two other programs not covered in the following reviews are: MagicIndex (Computer EdiType Systems) for CP/M, and

DocuMentor (PromptDoc, Inc.) for the Apple II with CP/M, which is part of a larger word processing program.

Most programs were written to integrate with the most popular program, WordStar. But as more word processing programs evolved, others appeared on the market. Perfect Writer and The FinalWord, for example, have an indexing program included with the word processor. MicroPro created its own program called StarIndex.

In addition to the programs mentioned, similar programs exist for other operating systems and word processing programs; some are in the public domain and may be downloaded for a specific system via the electronic bulletin boards with a modem. Software offerings change constantly; the programs reviewed will help you have insight into the programs' work "generally," and the results to expect. Watch ads and reviews for new programs and check the files of your local bulletin boards. Talk to people in a users' group to learn what programs they have found and that they find worthwhile.

INDEX Generator was written only to create an index so it is more limited than the others.

DOCUMATE/PLUS SETS THE SECTIONING AND GENERATES A TABLE OF CONTENTS

DocuMate/Plus asks only that you place a three dot command with a T (title or Tn [n] for number) after it above the heading to be indexed. On your screen the text will appear as:

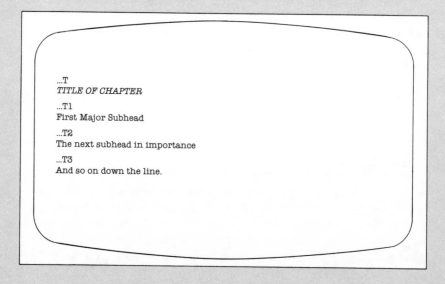

```
...T
TITLE OF CHAPTER
...T1
First Major Subhead
...T2
The next subhead in importance
...T3
And so on down the line.
```

When the TOC (table of contents) is requested in the menu, the page number and headings properly indented are generated in a new file now named FILENAME.TOC. They appear with the page number *preceding* the entry as:

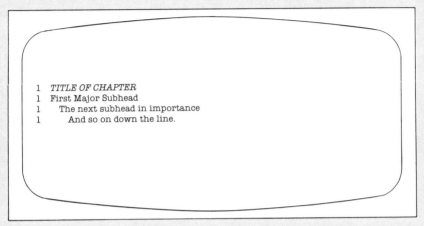

```
1   TITLE OF CHAPTER
1   First Major Subhead
1      The next subhead in importance
1        And so on down the line.
```

You can alter the default to change styles. For example, placing "...column width 44" at the top of the original file will yield page numbers *following* the entry. The location of the page number will be at the column width number you requested. Change the number and that's where it will appear as:

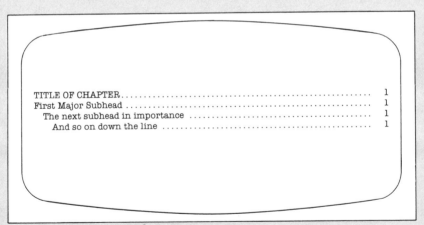

```
TITLE OF CHAPTER......................................................   1
First Major Subhead ...................................................   1
   The next subhead in importance ........................................   1
     And so on down the line ............................................   1
```

The program automatically makes a backup copy of the file it is reading. The resulting FILENAME.TOC (table of contents) file may be edited through WordStar and then printed.

DocuMate/Plus Indexing Procedures

Example: To index words in three lines of copy in sentences appearing on two separate pages would require you to put the dot directive

"...X," followed by the words to be indexed, *at the top of the page* or *above a line of copy containing the word.* On screen the prepared text would be:

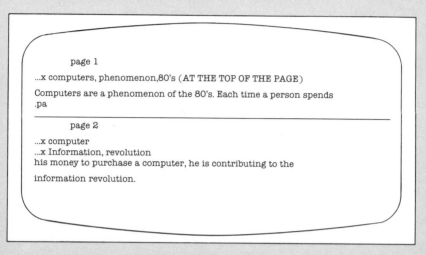

> page 1
>
> ...x computers, phenomenon,80's (AT THE TOP OF THE PAGE)
>
> Computers are a phenomenon of the 80's. Each time a person spends
> .pa
>
> page 2
>
> ...x computer
> ...x Information, revolution
> his money to purchase a computer, he is contributing to the
>
> information revolution.

To pull out the index, one returns to the menu, answers the necessary questions and lets the program go to work. A new file will be generated ready for editing or printing.

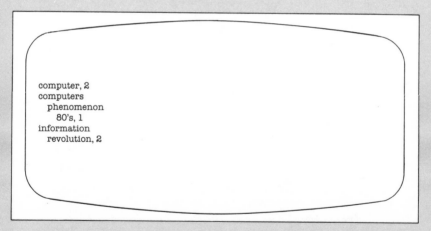

> computer, 2
> computers
>   phenomenon
>   80's, 1
> information
>   revolution, 2

Various formats and references may be accomplished using other dot directors such as R for reference, A for also, to become:

"...R" to produce
    80's, see *computer*
or "...A" to produce
    80's see also *computers, phenomenon*

Commas and quotation marks may also be included. After all indexed words are placed in a document, if you change page numbers with the .PN command or revise, DocuMate/Plus will pick up the new page number for the index. And only portions of a document can be redone if necessary. However, if reformatting text is necessary it must be done carefully or the result can be a total mess because dot commands may merge into the paragraphs.

Plus features are the ability to have cross references for any entry, and up to 8 levels of indexing where others allow one or two.

STARINDEX

StarIndex, a newcomer in the MicroPro line, offers welcome features for WordStar users only. It has a range of options lacking in other programs developed for WordStar integration. Yet none are exactly the same. Each has individual capabilities and you may prefer one over another.

StarIndex automatically styles headings but that styling is flexible. (Styling refers to which headings will be boldfaced, double printed, underlined, spaced, and other choices.) Perfect Writer styles a heading but it's not flexible. DocuMate lets you style the heading and you are responsible for consistency. It also gives you the choice as to whether and how sections should be numbered. (Perfect Writer does not let you eliminate or change the type of numbering in the major sectioning format.)

But each program described has other pros and cons. In StarIndex only one-line entries are allowed: A subhead that is longer than one line will be lopped off in the table of contents. It is possible to assign up to

As StarIndex reads a document it presents the new files it will produce along with a tally of the section and page numbers as it formats. If a level is skipped in the document, a warning bell beeps. Headings are marked for boldface or underlining and a table of contents file is produced with the extension .TOC.

```
MicroPro STARINDEX Release 1.01     Serial # IP3164PI
Copyright (c) 1983 MicroPro International Corporation
All rights reserved


        Format File Name: A:FORMAT.FMT
    Input Text File Name: B:CH1WORD.PRO
   Output Text File Name: B:CH1WORD.SI
Table of Contents File Name: B:CH1WORD.TOC
       Index File Name: B:CH1WORD.IDX


     Section      Page
     1. 7. 0. 0.      20 B:CH1WORD.PRO
Index Entries Read: 0
Index Entries Written: 0

StarIndex Complete

B0)_
```

256 characters for that line. In Perfect Writer, a long line will wrap around to a second line. None of these resulting inequities are hard to cope with because they may be changed with editing.

There are other considerations that may not be as easy to handle. StarIndex requires disk space for three additional files when it reads a document. It creates a new formatted copy of the document titled FILE-NAME.SI, a file with the table of contents titled FILENAME.TOC, and a file with the index titled FILENAME.IDX.

Directives for sectioning consist of only a period and two letters that are .IA, .IB, .IC, .ID. The combinations are used to indicate the main heading (.IA) and the B, C, D, for the second, third, and fourth levels. When the dot command is placed on the line before the heading, Star-Index will copy the heading to the table of contents. If a level is skipped the program will tell you so and you can return to the document to locate a heading you may have neglected to tag. On screen the headings are placed as:

```
.IA
THIS WOULD BE THE MAIN HEADING
.IB
This would be the Sub Heading
.IC
This would be the sub-subheading
Etc.
```

After formatting, the on-screen file would appear with the WordStar directives automatically added for underlining, boldface, and double printing. Anything could be deleted or changed in editing before printing.

```
                ^S^BT A B L E  O F  C O N T E T S^S^B
^D  1. THIS WOULD BE THE MAIN HEADING .......................... 2  ^D
^D     1.1 This would be the Sub Heading ...................... 3  ^D
^D        1.1.1 This would be the sub-subheading................. 3  ^D
```

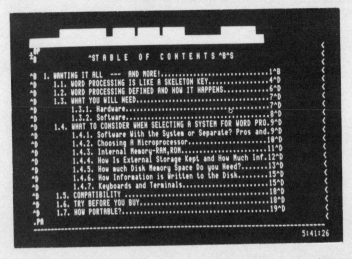

The table of contents generated by StarIndex will be keyed into the chapter titles as shown. Boldface, underline, and double print instructions can be deleted from the table of contents and the copy can be edited. Notice that line 1.4 was too long; missing words can be added as in any other text file.

The same procedures are followed for the appendices and for illustrations and tables but different letter combinations are used. .IE is for figures and .IT is for tables. (.IF is not used for figures because it is a command in the MailMerge program.)

There are additional convenient features in StarIndex. The format of the sections may be changed so numerals can be eliminated. Each title is a single line, but that line can be altered to 256 characters long. But more important is that any line can be tagged with an .IP and can summarize what is in a section. A table of contents entry could appear on screen as:

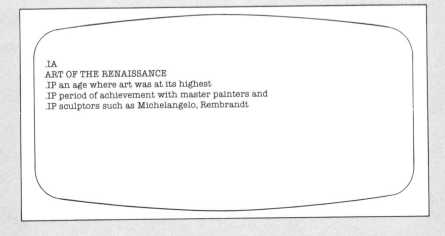

```
.IA
ART OF THE RENAISSANCE
.IP an age where art was at its highest
.IP period of achievement with master painters and
.IP sculptors such as Michelangelo, Rembrandt
```

Indexing

Indexing looks for two kinds of entries, those that are embedded in the text and those supplied by you.

If the words "bow and arrows" were already in the text, they could be sandwiched between commands and read for an index. They must be marked with either a ^P ^P at beginning and end for a general entry, or a ^P ^K at beginning and end for a master entry.

Entries supplied by you can contain some description. They can also be reversed and have a comma in the entry. An on-screen reference added by you would consist of an extra line inserted in the document as:

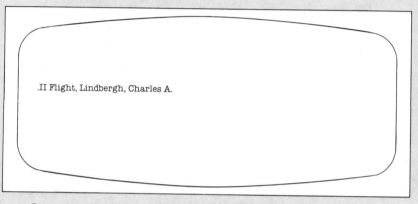

.II Flight, Lindbergh, Charles A.

On paper, in the final index it would appear as:

Flight

    Lindbergh, Charles, A.,   6

The program requires that .II (for Index) or .IM (for Master Index entry) be used. A Master entry on screen could be:

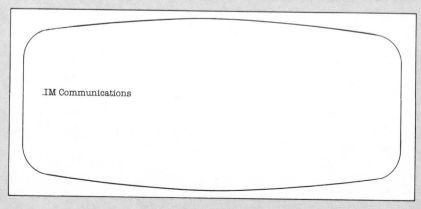

.IM Communications

On paper it would be:

Communications, **10**

The .IM command only boldfaces the page number. An explanation would be needed at the beginning of the index to let the reader know its meaning.

Shortcuts

Indexing the same word, or words, throughout a chapter or document can take time and it's possible to miss an entry. In any chapter, it would help to determine all entries you would want to list. Then use a global find and replace. For example, if you want to index all references to "flight," do a search for "flight" and insert a ".II flight" on each line preceding the word's appearance. Where feasible, use a find and replace to find a single word or short string and replace it with ^Pword^P or ^Kword^K.

Double Checking

To be sure you are indeed indexing everything that should be cited, any document could be run against Word Frequency in the spelling program THE WORD Plus, or using Profile in the program Grammatik (Chapter 4). The generated list of words could then be scanned for all the words to be indexed in each document. The "find" or "find and replace" procedures would be most efficient.

WORDINDEX HAS A DIFFERENT APPROACH

WordIndex is designed to be used *after* editing a document and *before* a final printout through WordStar. Think of it more as proofreaders' marks for a typesetter to follow than document sectioning. Once a document is set with the controls, further editing is difficult. Before subjecting a document through WordIndex, special dot commands are placed in the file. WordIndex then inserts the correct print directives based on these commands so it can number headings and subheadings. It automatically places underlines, boldface, and other WordStar print controls in the text. These same controls are used to generate a table of contents as in the other programs described.

WordIndex procedures for sectioning and generating a table of contents require a command with two dots followed by a masterspace "@" and a letter "A," "B," or "C" on the line above appropriate heads and subheads. In addition WordIndex permits you to place directives for boldface (b), underline (u), instead of pairs of controls used in WordStar (WS). Double spacing (s) between letters to space them out also can be requested.

Remember, WordIndex is meant to be used immediately before a document is printed. After you have added the print directives to set the table of contents, chapters, sections, and graphics, all will be numbered automatically for printout. If, after you run the document through WordIndex, you find you have missed something, a subsequent rerun can result in double entries. A safeguard backup file is recommended that should contain the original directives should a change be necessary. Mistakes are easy to make. The marked text would look like this on screen:

```
..@A b s             (indicates chapter, boldface, double space)
TITLE OF CHAPTER     (Title)
  In this chapter ....   (Text)
..@B
First Major Subhead
..@C
The next subhead in importance
..@A
SUBJECT INDEX
```

The program generates two new files. One is the formatted document, the other is the table of contents. All now contain the WordStar print directive with page numbers added.

On paper the above will print out as:

T A B L E   O F   C O N T E N T S

1. **TITLE OF CHAPTER** **3**
   1.1. First Major Subhead 3
      1.1.1. The Next subhead in importance 3
2. **SUBJECT INDEX** **3**

WordIndex Indexing

WordIndex generates an index at the end of the file as a result of your embedding double-dot commands for each word or two-word phrase you want in the index. The entry can be at the top of each page on which the terms appear or on a separate line above the entry. Only two levels of indexing can be accomplished using a ..@I directive for phrases and ..@M for master keyword entries. Figures and tables can be marked also. On screen index entries would appear as:

```
..@M Computer
..@I Computers, phenomenon 80's
Computers are a phenomenon of the 80's. Each time a person spends
.pa
_____

..@M Computer
..@M Money
..@I Information, revolution
 his money to purchase a computer, he is contributing to the
information revolution.
```

The subject index generated is alphabetized and the on-screen version appears as:

```
.cp5
C
_
Computer, 4, 5
.cp3
Computers
     phenomenon 80's, 4

.cp5
I
_
.cp3
Information
     revolution, 5

.cp5
M
_
Money, 5
```

The final printout of the index will be:

C
Computer, **4, 5**
Computers
    phenomenon 80's, 4
I
Information
    revolution, 5
M
Money, **5**

Documentation

WordIndex provides a printed manual that is generated by the program so you have an example of the final result. Two versions of the manual (before and after the text was modified by the program) are on disk files for on-screen viewing. Studying the placement of dot commands and marking the manual with the directives will serve as a visual reference. (You may discover many WordStar dot commands employed you may never think of using.)

Table titles, figure titles, and key words are kept in RAM, so the amount of RAM imposes a limit on the number of entries. With 64K of RAM, you can have about 700–800 different key words and approximately 25 figures and/or tables.

INDEX GENERATOR BY TOM JENNINGS

A program for indexing only, written by Tom Jennings, is in the public domain, available through the Boston bulletin board RCP/M (Remote CP/M).

INDEX Generator is delightfully easy to use. It, too, scans WordStar files for dot commands. The first must be "..index" at the top of the initial document page so INDEX Generator knows what it is looking for.

Only two directives are required: ^P^K and ^P^P, which show in the text as ^K and ^P.

^K is placed in front of each word to be indexed.

^P marks a phrase and must appear at the beginning and end of the phrase.

The on-screen text preparation would be:

```
                              page 1
^KComputers are a ^K phenomenon of the ^K80's. Each time a person spends
.pa
                              page 2
   his ^Kmoney to purchase a computer, he is contributing to the
^Pinformation revolution^P.
```

The subject index will appear at the end of the text and print out as hard copy:

INDEX Generator works within a new file it names INDEXI and the original is in the backup. It sorts in ASCII * order with digits, quotes, and parentheses appearing before letters. Each entry will begin with a capital letter.

This program generates a one-level index only. It would be practical to use in conjunction with a spelling program that marks the front of a word. As with StarIndex, a list of words could be generated for indexing, then those words found and replaced with the necessary command letter ^K and ^P added. Any duplications in the index could be deleted during editing.

If headings and subheads were sandwiched in ^K ^K commands, a crude table of contents could be created, then edited to a style the user likes.

---

* ASCII stands for American Standard Code for Information Interchange ("as-key"). It provides numerical equivalents for the alphabet, numbers, punctuation, and special symbols.

PERFECT WRITER

Perfect Writer and The FinalWord share the same procedures for sectioning documents. Each program counts prestyled "formats" among its virtues. They require a variety of @ sign placements and ENVIRON-MENT commands.

Options provide some flexibility but if you have a definite idea of how you wish a document to appear and that final form is not provided in the program, you won't be able to generate it automatically. If you can bend your ideas to the program's output, the result is acceptable for many purposes. The advantage of these two programs is that the features are included, the same idea as "standard equipment" on a car. The stand alone programs for WordStar are "optional extras." None are inter-changeable or compatible with other word processing programs.

The options and their commands may be applied to documents from a few pages up to a full book, depending upon the format. There is a style for unnumbered two-level sectioning and another that generates numbered headings and subheadings and another series for four-level sectioning.

The style may also include a heading that is centered, boldfaced, or underlined. Once you declare a style, you can't change it in that docu-ment. Spacing between headings and text, and beginning a chapter on a new page are among the automatic aspects of the form.

Unnumbered Two-Level Headings or Numbered Four-Level Headings

For an unnumbered heading, commands placed on screen would appear as:

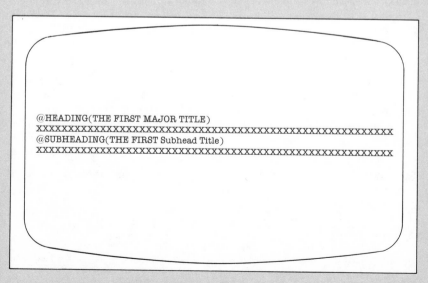

```
@HEADING(THE FIRST MAJOR TITLE)
XXXXXXXXXXXXXXXXXXXXXXXXXXXXXXXXXXXXXXXXXXXXXXXXXXXXXXXXX
@SUBHEADING(THE FIRST Subhead Title)
XXXXXXXXXXXXXXXXXXXXXXXXXXXXXXXXXXXXXXXXXXXXXXXXXXXXXXXXX
```

It will appear on paper as:

THE FIRST MAJOR TITLE

XXXXXXXXXXXXXXXXXXXXXXXXXXXXXXXXXXXXXXXXXXXXXXXXXXXXXXXX
XXXXXXXXXXXXXXXXXXXXXXXXXXXXXXXXXXXXXXXXXXXXXXXXXXXXXXXX
XXXXXXXXXXXXXXXXXXXXXXXXXXXXXXXXXXXXXXXXXXXXXXXXXXXXXXXX

THE FIRST Subhead Title

XXXXXXXXXXXXXXXXXXXXXXXXXXXXXXXXXXXXXXXXXXXXXXXXXXXXXXXX
XXXXXXXXXXXXXXXXXXXXXXXXXXXXXXXXXXXXXXXXXXXXXXXXXXXXXXXX

Numbered Four-Level Sectioning with Appendices

Another format will yield relational numbered four-level sectioning plus an appendix. The same numbered titles appear in a table of contents. The document may be indexed and it will include page references. Both the table of contents and the index may be placed in another file for editing.

Very long documents must be broken into smaller sections (such as chapters or portions of chapters) for the program to work efficiently and smoothly. But they can be chained together. Other commands within the program must be placed to generate consecutive chapter numbering.

The wealth of tools built into these word processors probably offer the most comprehensive programs for sectioning documents in any word processors around.

The Index Program

Perfect Writer's own index program is the only one that can be used with it. A single level entry is generated; major and sublevel subjects cannot be differentiated. It does not have the same flexibility or ease of use as the stand alone indexing programs combined with WordStar.

Each word to be indexed must be enclosed between parentheses with the appropriate @INDEX command preceding it. That opens up a margin for many errors because of the extra typing and command placement required.

Another problem is that Perfect Writer does not show page breaks; therefore every occurrence of an entry must be marked, compared with a program that shows page breaks where marking only a single occurrence on any page would be sufficient.

Here's how two paragraphs would appear on screen with words tagged for indexing:

Imagine being able to tag words and phrases throughout a @INDEX<document> and have them appear at the end of the text completely @INDEX<alphabetized> and @INDEX<numbered>, by pages to result in an index. It's the @INDEX<computerized> method of eliminating "index" cards ... the original reason such cards were developed.

The use of @@INDEX is designed for long @INDEX<documents>. It can be used on short documents and on any and all documents—not only those in which numbered headings are used such as @INDEX<chapters>, @INDEX<paragraphs>, and so forth. It will create an @INDEX<alphabetical> listing on any length document. Try it on a sample to understand its @INDEX<mechanics>.

Below is the generated index showing actual position of numbers. The file is added to the end of the document but it can be moved to another file and edited.

Index

alphabetical 30
alphabetized 30
chapters 30
computerized 30
document 30
documents 30
mechanics 30
numbered 30
paragraphs 30

Whether one of these programs fits your needs is a decision only you can make. The present programs can be advantageous for sectioning and automatically generating a table of contents. For an index, an inordinate amount of time may be needed to prepare a lengthy document— and this must be weighed against the time it might take to generate the output in the old-fashioned (shhhh) ways. The goals are admirable but I'll continue to watch for a better way to generate an index than retyping or flagging words on every page of a document.

COMPARISON CHART OF PROGRAMS

	DOCUMATE	STARINDEX	PERFECT WRITER	WORD INDEX	INDEX GENERATOR
SECTIONING					
No. of levels	16	4	4	3	
Chapter	yes	yes	yes		
Section	yes	yes	yes		
Subsection	yes	yes	yes		
Paragraph	yes	yes	yes		
Appendix		yes	no		
Appendix Section		yes	no	no	
REFERENCES:					
Tables	no	yes	no	yes	
Figures	no	yes	no	yes	
NUMBERS GENERATED	no	optional	yes		
STYLE OPTIONS	yes	yes	no	no	
TABLE OF CONTENTS	yes	yes	yes	yes	
Entry length limit	1 line	1 line	no	no limit	
Text entry allowed	no	yes	no	no	
PRINT DIRECTIVES					
Can style be changed?	yes	yes	no	yes	
Boldface	yes	yes	yes		
Double strike	yes	yes	yes		
Elongated print	no	yes	no		
Underline	yes	yes	yes		
Normal print	yes	yes	no		
INDEX					
No. of levels	8	2	1	2	1
Line length limit	1 line	1 line	40 characters	1 line	1 line
ON-SCREEN EXAMPLES	yes	yes	yes	yes	yes
MANUAL	good	excellent	good	good	good
SUPPORT SYSTEMS	CP/M	CP/M;MSDOS	CP/M;MSDOS	CP/M	CP/M
PRICE		$195 WordStar compatible	included with Perfect Writer	$395	Public Domain

The above programs are representative of the way most programs work. More word processing programs will continue to include these features in their package.

COMPANIES AND PROGRAMS

☐ DOCUMATE/PLUS
The Orthocode Corporation
Distributed by
Lifeboat Associates
1651 Third Ave.
New York, NY 10028
(212)860-0300

CP/M -Z80 or 8080. 5¼- and 8-inch disks
Disk K = .COM file 26K. Documentation 28K.
Requires 48K.
PRICE $175

☐ STARINDEX
MicroPro International Corp.
33 San Pablo Ave.
San Rafael, CA 94903
(415) 499-1200

CP/M, PCDOS, MSDOS.
PRICE $195

☐ WORDINDEX
Release #3.0 Jan. 1981
Modulare Intelligenta Data Administrations Systemer
Lifeboat Associates
1651 Third Ave.
New York, NY 10028
(212) 860-0300

CP/M, Z80 or 8080. 5¼- and 8-inch
PRICE $395

☐ SAMNA WORD III
Samna Corp.
2700 NE Expressway
Building C Street 700
Atlanta, GA 30345
(800) 241-2065
PCDOS, MSDOS-320K.
Included in word processing.
PRICE $550

☐ INDEX GENERATOR
Tom Jennings
For CP/M -Z80 or 8080
Distributed by
RCP/M system Boston (Remote CP/M Bulletin Board)
Paul Kelly (617) 862-0781

The program is in the public domain, but exclusive ownership is retained by Tom Jennings. Anyone can use or give it away, but not sell it. It may be added to CP/M users' group libraries.
DISK K = .COM file 10K. Documentation 20K.
Requires 48K. Any disk size.
Free via RCP/M BOSTON.

☐ MAGICINDEX
Computer EdiType Systems
509 Cathedral Pkwy.
New York, NY 10025
(212) 222-8148

CP/M.
Versions for WordStar, Electric Pencil, Magic Wand, Mince, P/Mate, Select and Word Master.
PRICE $150

☐ FIRSTDRAFT
PromptDoc, Inc.
833 W. Colorado Ave.
Colorado Springs, CO 80905
(303) 471-9875

For Apple II with CP/M. The indexing feature is part of the word processing program.
PRICE $195

8. Using Spreadsheet Programs for Text Entry

ou have been introduced to a variety of programs that take you into and beyond the phenomenon of basic word processing. Is it all so wondrous? Is there a hitch somewhere? Is there some task that is difficult to accomplish even with the power of the word processor?

Well. Yes. But another category program used creatively can overcome that.

Creating charts and odd page formats with a word processor often requires time-consuming gyrations. It's hard to write copy that fits "around" a picture when you want to use the computer's output for a final presentation (as opposed to sending material to a typesetter).

Finalizing such formats is not so easy with a majority of word processing programs. You can use tabulation to create text columns or math table input (if a program has it). But when you think you have all the columns and rows ready you may decide to change one entry; suddenly, all other rows reformat and undo what you've struggled to accomplish. Or perhaps your program won't extend beyond the width of your terminal's screen. It's possible, too, to reedit and forget to change a word wrap or justification command. The computer never knows what you "meant" to do, it only follows your instructions. Any number of conditions can cause carefully setup columns to rearrange instantaneously into oddly spaced paragraphs. It's pull-out-your-hair time!

Only a few programs have the capability of formatting text in columns. Columns could be typed separately, then each column moved into a proper position if the program has a column move capability. But lining them up could be a hassle when there are many columns. Without such a feature it is possible to play around with the way you input information until you get it just right. But the difficulties are too great to contemplate. At times like this the old cut, paste, and photocopy it all into one method is a decided attraction.

The program MagicPrint, and its sister program MagicBind (see pages 81 and 167), will output type into two and three columns or more, by placing a series of dot commands in the file. Essentially they fool the computer into thinking it's a typesetter, but you must have a certain daisy wheel printer or a specific NEC Spinwriter, and one of seven word processing programs that are compatible with all the requirements. They are superb programs but the parameters are like having the moon in the third quarter with no clouds in the sky between 1 and 2 A.M.

What if you don't have *all* those conditions operating at the right time? Are there ways to get around some of the limitations?

Absolutely.

A spreadsheet program, also referred to as a "calc" program, will overcome many limitations of a word processing program. Calc programs are associated with mathematical "calculations" for accounting. They carry names such as VisiCalc, SuperCalc, CalcStar, Perfect Calc, Multicalc, MasterCalc, MagiCalc, Lotus 1-2-3, etc.

How can such a program perform word processing feats?

With ingenuity, and some practice, you can enter text in myriad ways for special formats. They are perfect when you need to create charts or columns you would be struggling with from now till doomsday using the basic word processor. All the comparison charts in this book are an example. Each was prepared using the text entry capability within SuperCalc2.

Basically, a spreadsheet, as generated by a calc program, is not much different from the kind of entries you would use for your own checkbook, a household budget, or in keeping track of expenses for your income tax report. It is simply a rectangular grid of lines and columns, like a large sheet of graph paper, onto which data can be entered. These programs have the capability of accepting text instead of numbers in each "cell" of their simulated spreadsheet. Cells can be altered to accommodate different length entries up to about 127 characters (depending on the program). You can enter titles the full width of the proposed chart and as many rows vertically as the program will provide.

After the chart is completed, you can eliminate the "border" of numerals and letters when you are ready to print. The chart can be printed through the calc program or it can be saved into a disk in a file that a word processor can understand. That allows you to edit it, put it through a spelling program, change the pitch or type size, and incorporate it into a text file.

Here's how a checkbook entry would appear in an electronic spreadsheet:

	A || B ||	C	|| D || E || F	
1	CheckRegister							
2				Thursday 8/1/85				
3								
4	Check				Check	Deposit		
5	Number		Date	Description	Amount	Amount		Balance
6								
7				Beginning Balance				$1,150.00
8		2000		Phone Company	930.00			$220.00
9		2001		Cleaners	140.00			$80.00
10		2002		Department Store	100.00			($20.00)
11						250.00		$230.00
12		2003		Pharmacy	65.00			$165.00
13		2004		Electric Company	250.00			($85.00)
14						900.00		$815.00
15								
16								
17								
18								

Each numerical entry and each text entry is placed in a "cell." Another way to state it is that each "cell" contains one unit of information. Instead of numbers, imagine filling each cell with short text. Commands for working a spreadsheet program are too complex to cover here. One usually buys a calc program for other procedures than text entry. The integrated programs that combine three or more business procedures, such as Lotus 1-2-3, will make the task easier.

If you plan to use a calc program for its prime purpose as well as some text entry, you should look for the following features.

1. Can the entry be "protected" so it can't be deleted or moved without "unprotecting"?
2. Are entries easy to delete and edit individually as well as by rows and columns?
3. Can information in one cell be repeated with a copy or edit command?
4. Can cell sizes be easily altered?
5. Can the program accept titles? What lengths?
6. Can the program generate an ASCII file that can be edited by any word processor? Or only the word processor with which it is compatible?
7. When printing directly from the calc program, can the numerical borders be eliminated and the format changed so that it can be single- or double-spaced?

8. Can text entries be justified right and left?
9. Does the program provide adequate capacity for the size and kind of charts you may wish to design? Some programs have limits as to the number of rows and columns and the number of digits possible in each cell.

GENERATING A CHART WITH A SPREADSHEET PROGRAM

The example of the checkbook and the photo of the calc program taken from the screen show how a border with rows and columns appears. They simplify placing entries in the proper columns and rows. Any space may be left blank until you are sure of the correct entry; you can go back and fill in or change the information in any cell. Rows and columns can be inserted and deleted. They can be moved from one place to another by any increments from a single cell to any size portion of the chart. They are extremely versatile and reliable.

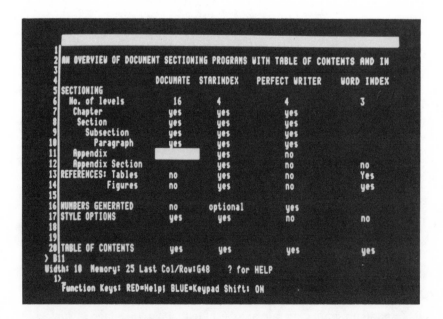

A text chart is much easier to create in a spreadsheet program than in a word processing program unless special column entry features are offered. Even then, a word processing program may not handle text information as well as a spreadsheet program. Alphabetical and numerical borders simplify entry placements; entries can be locked so they can't be moved accidentally. The borders can be eliminated when printed.

Here is how the portion of the chart shown in the photo above appears without the border numbers and letters.

AN OVERVIEW OF DOCUMENT SECTIONING PROGRAMS WITH TABLE OF CONTENTS	DOCUMATE	PERFECT WRITER	STARINDEX	WORDINDEX
SECTIONING				
No. of levels	16	4	4	3
Chapter	yes	yes	yes	
Section	yes	yes	yes	
Subsection	yes	yes	yes	
Paragraph	yes	yes	yes	
Appendix		no	yes	
Appendix Section		no	yes	no
REFERENCES: Tables	no	no	yes	yes
Figures	no	no	yes	yes
NUMBERS GENERATED	no	yes	optional	yes
STYLE OPTIONS	yes	no	yes	
TABLE OF CONTENTS	yes	yes	yes	yes
Entry Length Limit	1 line	no	1 line	1 line

After a program is saved on disk as a word processing file, entry protection is overridden and it may be edited as though it had originated in the word processing program.

A spreadsheet program will also let you format around pictures and set up columns when a word processing program does not have these capabilities. More often, the combination of spreadsheet and word processing will facilitate odd formatting and defy the limitations of either or both programs. Integrated programs with several modules can also be investigated for their multicapabilities.

COMPANIES AND PROGRAMS

□ **SUPERCALC 2 and SUPERCALC 3**
Sorcim Corp.
2310 Lindy Ave.
San Jose, CA 95131
(408) 942-1727

CP/M, PCDOS, MSDOS.

□ **LOTUS 1-2-3 and SYMPHONY**
Lotus Development Corp.
55 Wheeler St.
Cambridge, MA 02138
(800) 343-5414
(617) 492-7870 (MA)

PCDOS, MSDOS.

NOTE: Because offerings change so quickly for these programs, please refer to advertisements for current list and discount prices.

9. Merge Programs Expand Word Processing Power

 "merge" program combined with word processing is the answer to the prayers of any typist who has ever had to send the same letter to several, possibly hundreds of, people. For those who wished that each letter would appear personalized, a mail merge program could spell heaven when properly implemented. Each "form" letter can be addressed to a specific individual as though it were customized. Indeed, it can be customized, though still a form letter.

You probably have received dozens of similar mailings in which your name appears at the top of the letter and again in the body of the text. (Subscribe to such and such a magazine, Mrs. Jones.) Each one, of perhaps a mailing of thousands, is a form letter, though addressed and with a salutation to each recipient.

WHAT SHOULD A MERGE PROGRAM ACCOMPLISH?

A merge program should be able to handle lists and put them together with a master document during the print process. But many programs can accomplish much more. A merge program should:

1. Automatically combine any files or portions of files for lists or for boilerplate letters.

2. Allow you to interact with a form letter and add to it just before it is printed should you wish to further customize a specific letter.
3. Let you chain print several files one after another.
4. Nest one file within another.
5. Select portions of a list for printing . . . called "conditional printing."
6. Let you see the document as it is being printed if you desire.
7. Print multiple copies.
8. Allow you to reformat a document at print time.

How is this magic performed? Not as magic at all, but by planning ahead. In mailing list handling, one file contains the master letter. Another file contains the names and addresses as a "data base" that is simply a mailing list or other record list. The master letter contains a set of commands that does the directing and the printer produces the final output.

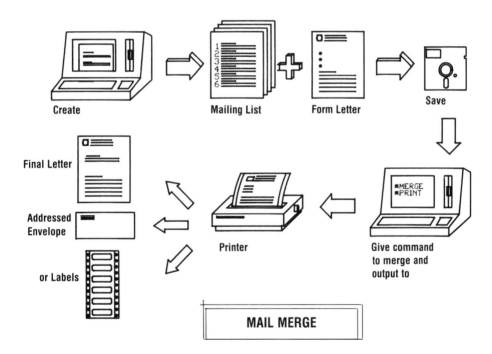

The user prepares a mailing list and a form matrix letter and places each in a file on disk. Next he creates a "command file" which tells the program to take the letter from its file and take one address at a time from its file, put them together, and send them to the printer. The printer assembles the information into the form it has been told to use and produces the final letters, envelopes, or labels.

WHERE DO YOU FIND THESE PROGRAMS?

Merge programs that will accomplish some or all of the above almost always work only with a parent word processing program because commands used must be integrated and compatible. Generically they may be referred to as mail merge programs but occasionally they are couched under another title.

Among word processing software that includes, or has an optional mail merge program, are Perfect Writer, MegaWriter, MultiMate, Easytext, Select, SuperWriter, Wordnet, Word Perfect, WordPlus, WordStar, Word II, Write-On!, and others. As new programs are introduced and users expect and demand this capability, companies will strive to include it. Before you invest in a word processing program, decide whether you need merge features; if so, be sure to purchase a program that will do the merge procedures you need.

There are a few stand alone programs that have merge capability. MagicBind's main thrust is to produce customized format printing but it includes merge procedures in its routines. Versions are available to integrate with several specific word processing programs and to be used with Diablo and NEC Spinwriter printers.

WHO WOULD USE SUCH A PROGRAM?

There are many facets to a full feature merge program and different people would use some or all for different reasons. Here are a few.

In an office monthly billings to the same customers are sent using a computerized mailing list that resides in one or more files. A statement is prepared each month and the customer's name is automatically inserted on the appropriate statement.

Church officers may mail monthly newsletters, occasional special announcements, and biannual letters to solicit donations. Only one mailing list is needed and it can be merged with whichever document is required for that specific mailing. If the biannual solicitation letter must include each member's name at the top of the letter as Dear Mr. Jones, that, too, can be accomplished with the same list without any retyping.

A public relations company sends out releases to various media representatives. The same mailing list can be used for every mailing. They can sort the list into types of media contacts, perhaps those for TV, some for newspapers, magazines, and radio, and send each a different version of the mailing.

People who prepare long documents, such as reports or books, could work with short portions of the manuscript, then print them as one full manuscript using the "chaining" tool.

Boilerplate letters are so named because, in the days of typesetting, certain paragraphs were set up as a mat or a block of type. They could be plunked in where needed without resetting. In computer terms, boilerplate has a similar connotation except that it refers to stock paragraphs kept in files that can be merged into correspondence whenever needed. Stock paragraphs are stock-in-trade for attorneys, professional people, and anyone who must use the same form letter with only slight variations.

In the home, greeting card recipients could be kept in a file. The total list might be used at Christmas: individual names could be pulled out and used as needed for other occasions.

WHAT DO YOU HAVE TO DO?

Mail merge programs simplify work, but the user still must feed in the proper information to make it all happen. The program does only what it is told to do.

The user must:

1. Create a master "matrix" letter in one file with specific directives at the places where "variables" will be inserted. Different programs use different symbols. The following example is from MailMerge and WordStar.

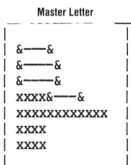

Master Letter

A master letter is written as a matrix. The &...& signs will be replaced by the name, address, etc., or the "fields" established in the mailing list with which it will be merged.

2. The user prepares a record list, usually a mailing list, in a second file. This list is prepared with the word processing program according to specific rules such as commas between each part or "field" in the list, and no hard carriage returns.

A "field" is one part of the entry set off from another by commas; a name, address, city, etc. A field in an address list also is referred to as a "variable value" in the form letter.

1st field	2nd field	3rd field	4th field	5th field	6th field
1,	Doris Dayton,	President,	Dayton Cosmetics,	1 Ageless St.,	Everywhere CA 92000

3. The user establishes a command file that tells the program to look for a specific field in the list and to position that field in the master letter.

The command file contains only those instructions that tell the other files how to proceed. It is like a music conductor directing portions of the orchestra to play their parts at different times and then together.

Names and addresses need never be retyped once they are placed in a record file. The same list or portions of the list can be used indefinitely for as many different pieces of correspondence and as often as one needs it.

Ask For Variables While Printing

The user can also request that a variable be ASKED FOR during printing. When the variable command is placed in the master document, at the place where different wording is to be printed, a prompt appears on screen at printing time. The printer pauses and waits until the user adds the information. Perhaps a new name and address will need to be inserted into each letter. It could be an amount of money, the title of a book, the name of a product. Any number of situations can require adding data individually to a letter as it is being printed. The "Ask for Variable" is the tool that will accomplish this task.

Labels, Envelopes

The same record, or data, file with addresses may be used to output the list on mailing labels in different formats by changing the directives, or creating a command file giving the margins desired, the number of lines, and the spacing between lines. Then when you are ready to print, you request the command file that holds the label data, and the same list you used to head a letter now prints out the label.

One command file can be established to print the data onto continuous form single labels or to write them three across. Another series of commands will set up the printing for envelopes, but you, or a special envelope feeder machine, will have to insert the envelopes.

It is also possible to alternate the printing of a letter and an envelope so there is less chance of mixing up who gets which letter. When labels and letters are printed separately, one must be careful to coordinate the addressee's letter with the proper envelope.

Chaining—for Combining Documents in Separate Files

Merge programs can accomplish much more than the time-saving ability to print names and addresses into multiple copies of a master document.

In some businesses it is essential to use master letters with an assortment of different paragraphs for various recipients. The letters vary but use boilerplate paragraphs. In this situation, the files would be chained so one prints after another. The same procedure would be used by the report or book author to chain together sections or chapters of a manuscript.

Nesting Paragraphs and Files

Sometimes it will be convenient to request that a paragraph, set up as a file, be inserted within a document rather than using the chaining procedure described above. This is called "nesting." Nesting lets you put an entire file inside another, and perhaps another inside that and still another inside that one . . . up to as many as seven times in one printing. You are telling your printer, "I've put a command in the letter that says 'get another file and print it here before you continue with this file.' "

Conditional Printing

Conditional printing is a sophisticated procedure that appears in some programs but not all. It establishes a "condition" that permits you to be selective as you request printing. It acts as a type of "sort" program in that you can choose to place some text in some form letters but have it omitted from others . . . all during the same print output.

When would such a tool be used?

If you are a dentist, you might have a form letter that tells some patients that *if* their teeth need cleaning on the next visit, they should make an appointment, *except* for those who have had it done within the past six months.

If your company is raising funds, a letter might specify "except for donors who gave more than $1,000 last year" and then the program would be told to ignore the last paragraphs of the letter.

The procedure requires using IF and EXcept concepts. A conditional command could state, "If the zip code is 94111, go to the second paragraph and print." The command file has to contain specific information so that MailMerge knows what to skip when it is given the clue.

Other Programs May Vary in Operation

Merge programs appear more complex than they really are once you are familiar with them. Some software includes similar capabilities within a program and does not necesssarily refer to the tools by the same terminology. Often they are called "boilerplate letter and form letter" features.

Whatever mail merge program you select to expand your word processor's capabilities, you'll discover that it can offer exciting procedures for accomplishing many correspondence and writing tasks more efficiently.

MAILING LIST MANAGEMENT PROGRAMS WITHOUT MERGING

There are programs designed only to manage mailing lists for users who do not require the list to be merged with a document. Or they will optionally allow the list to be merged with a specific program. Almost any and every sophisticated data base program can accomplish this task, such as dBase II by Ashton Tate.

But less complex programs are available that are specifically designed for the purpose. Such a program may also let you establish "identifiers" by which you may sort the list into specific groups. They also simplify editing an entry. Look for these programs in magazines under headings of "Mailing List Software."

If merge software, or straight mailing list programs, will serve your needs, make a list of what you would want to accomplish, then check program advertisements and compare the features offered against your wish list. Ask your software dealer for recommendations. People who run mailing list services and secretaries in offices might also offer valid recommendations, and criticism of bad features, and praise for those that are worthwhile. There's no substitute for conducting your own surveys.

Creating data bases is a subject covered by entire books and usually not mentioned as a word processing adjunct, but when the need is there, the two go together as hand and glove.

COMPANIES AND PROGRAMS

☐ MAILMERGE
MicroPro International Corp.
33 San Pablo Ave.
San Rafael, CA 94903
(415) 499-1200
PRICE $250

☐ MICROMAILER
P.O. Box 2802
La Jolla, CA 92038
(619) 455-7442

CP/M only, certain machines.
PRICE $89.95

☐ NOTEBOOK by PRO/TEM
Digital Marketing Corp.
2363 Boulevard Circle
Walnut Creek, CA 94595
(800) 826-2222
PRICE $150

☐ dBASE II + dBASE III
Ashton-Tate
10150 W. Jefferson Blvd.
Culver City, CA 90230
(213) 204-5570
PRICE $700

10. Hard Copy— Printers and Their Peripherals

There are rumblings and predictions that the computer will result in a paperless society. Less paper is probable. But no paper? Very unlikely. And unthinkable! Can you imagine reading everything from a computer terminal? No more books to hold in your hand under a soft light in bed at night. (How does one curl up with a good terminal?) No more newspapers to spread out under a coffee cup at breakfast. Nothing to recycle, except perhaps used floppy disks. Horrors!

A printer or some other hard copy device is essential to capture the thoughts trapped in the magnetic oxide ridges and send them on to their ultimate audience. (Unless some visionaries see things differently.)

There are many choices for making hard copy and the selection will increase. Therefore, it helps to organize what's available so you can make a decision as to the best device for your purposes. It isn't necessary to buy a printer that a salesperson insists is "right" for any computer. If you purchased a printer early in the game, it's possible you may want a different unit, or more than one. There are also plotters, formerly a high-ticket item with lower-cost versions now available.

The variety, price range, and features of output devices change at such a rapid rate that discussion of specific units is quickly outdated.

Another problem is interfacing printers, computers, and software so they all work in perfect harmony. You'll hear references to "patching" software so it will take advantage of all the capabilities the printer has to offer.

Arranging the pins of the connectors to be compatible with the I/O (input/output) ports on the computer can produce problems for which there are not always easy solutions. Some of these problems are sufficiently common that they have spawned entire business services.

If you're not absolutely sure specific hardware and software will work the way you want it to, you will have to do your own research. If dealers are vague, or give "maybe" and "it should" answers, don't accept those as gospel. Many printers will not work with some computers. Some software will not perform properly with some printers and computers. Different cables and RS232 pin configurations may be needed. It's not unusual to have equipment sit idle for months until someone figures out the right combinations. Question people at users' groups, ask if others have had good or bad experiences making all of the same products work properly together. If you find the right answers to the problems before you buy you'll save yourself headaches and frustrations.

Be prepared for noise with an "impact" type printer. An impact printer is one with tiny hammers that strike a character on an element that hits the paper, or with tiny hammers that hit the paper directly. You'll find these on letter quality printers and dot matrix printers. Thermal and ink jet printers are not guilty of noise but they have other drawbacks.

Beyond that, there are many "peripherals" for the printer, such as spoolers, switchers, labelers, and more which you will see in ads and supply catalogs. There are many choices of ready to use papers and forms for every type of output. All expand your word processing power.

TYPES OF OUTPUT DEVICES

Anything that takes data from the computer and places it where it can be seen, and used, is an output device. The terminal allows you to read data only while it is on. Hard copy is the permanent output; a printer is one device for producing that hard copy.

Letter Quality Printers

When the written word is involved (as opposed to graphics) the typed image may be set down on paper using different technologies. A "letter quality" printer produces a character composed of a solid line as you see in this print and as a conventional typewriter prints. The actual print impact is made by an element shaped like a daisy wheel or a thimble. Each fully formed letter is raised on one of the stems of the element and the image is impacted by a tiny hammer that strikes it and sends the image through the ribbon onto the paper. It's all done so rapidly the eye cannot follow it happening.

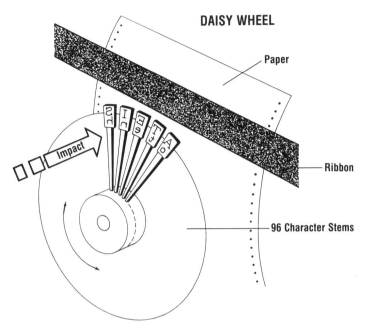

DAISY WHEEL

Paper

Ribbon

96 Character Stems

A daisy wheel element produces an "impact" print. A tiny hammer strikes a stem with a letter on it. The letter hits the ribbon and imprints the image on the paper.

A daisy wheel letter quality printer, one of the Diablo 630 series. Print speed is 40 characters per second (cps) and some graphics can be integrated with text. It will accept fanfold and sheet feed paper. By changing the print element different units can produce up to 200 print styles, including 33 languages, plus scientific, mathematical, and legal fonts.

Courtesy of Diablo Systems Inc., A Xerox Company

A good letter quality printer will usually print from 15 to 55 characters per second (cps). Lower-priced units may print only 7 to 14 characters per second. One difference is that high quality faster printers move the element back and forth or "bidirectionally" so it places type on the paper as it moves from left to right and right to left. Less expensive and slower printers may print in only one direction, or "unidirectionally."

A fast typist working on a conventional typewriter can produce perhaps 8 to 10 cps, and may slip in a few typos. Fifteen cps is faster than most people type. At 15 cps, with an average of 6 letters per word, the result would be 90 words per minute, and no errors. At 55 cps, the errorless result (providing all errors were corrected on the terminal prior to printing) would come to 330 words per minute. A 2,000-word, double-spaced, 10-page document would require only 6 minutes. Fast. Yes. But many dot matrix printers can produce characters much faster.

Dot Matrix Printers

Each character formed by a dot matrix printer is composed of tiny dots similar to the way it appears on the terminal screen. Speeds range from about 60 to 220 characters per second. Because each dot is the result of a single hammer strike, an infinite variety of images can be formed compared to the preformed letters on a letter quality printer. Therefore, with the proper software, a dot matrix printer may be able to produce characters of different alphabets and an endless assortment of graphic images. Because of the difference in speed between letter quality and dot matrix printers, some offices use both types. A dot matrix may be used for draft quality printing and for billing: the letter quality may be used for more formal correspondence and for final copy of certain types of text.

A Durango dot matrix printer is offered with the POPPY personal computer system. It features variable printing speeds up to 218 cps with a flexible choice of font styles and graphics.
Courtesy of Durango Systems, Inc.

Even that is changing as the quality of dot matrix printers improves and the dots print more closely together. Manufacturers of dot matrix printers offer a "correspondence quality" mode. What does that mean? By requesting that each dot "double print" the dotted line fills in more solidly and the result simulates a solid line rather than a dotted line. Double printing slows down the process and cuts the speed in half, but for many purposes the result is adequate. It can mean that the dot matrix printer doubles its function and its value for considerably less than a letter quality printer. And only one unit is required; a saving in space as well as money.

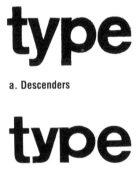

a. Descenders

b. No Descenders

Type with and without descenders.

The type style that a dot matrix can create and the size of the letters are important. Another concern is that the characters "g," "j," "p," "q," "y" have "true descenders." That means that the portions below the baseline of each of these letters descends below the line.

There are some matrix printers that will support both graphics and color so that images and text can be combined.

Electronic Typewriters—Computer Printers

In the early days of computer output devices, electric and electronic typewriters were converted and sometimes combined to serve as both typewriter and computer output device. Generally, they performed neither job well and the original typewriter, not made for the hard driving repeat impact of a computer, broke down frequently.

Recently, several companies created electronic machines specifically designed to double as a conventional typewriter and also switch to become a letter quality computer output device. Speeds are slow, ranging from 7 to 14 cps. Prices are attractive but early reports are that they need more improvement. For minimal hard copy output, and in situations where both types of machines are needed, these units may warrant consideration. They will undoubtedly improve in the future.

Thermal Printers

Thermal printers have been on the market for some time but have not normally been associated with word processing. Thermal paper is costly and the type tends to fade after a few months. How does the thermal printer work? Characters are created by selectively heating pins of a dot matrix printhead. The heat darkens the coated paper in dot shapes that form the character matrix. Therefore the printheads, or hammers, never touch the paper and printing is silent. The print quality is mediocre and speeds are slow. Carbons cannot be achieved because the print is not made by an impact procedure.

Ink Jet Printers

Ink jet printers, like thermal printers, do not use an impact device so they, too, are quiet. They cannot produce a carbon. Instead of the pin or hammer device, ink jet printers use ink-filled channels that spray liquid ink in a continuous stream or a drop at a time depending upon the system.

Newer, low-cost ink jet printers employ a "drop on demand" technique that uses ink cartridges that feed the ink into several nozzles. When pressure is applied selectively to each nozzle, a drop of ink is ejected and deposited on the paper.

The Canon color ink jet printer can produce 7 colors on both plain paper and overhead transparencies. It has 4 different character styles and prints at 37 cps. It is a "drop on demand" technology with two separate, large capacity ink cartridges; one black and one tricolor.
Courtesy of Canon USA, Inc.

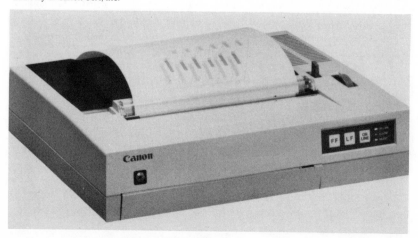

Technology surrounding ink jet printers is constantly improving. The problems? A high quality, slick surface paper must be used for best results; normal bond paper may cause the ink to spread and get fuzzy at the characters' edges. Ink jet printer nozzles tend to clog, although new techniques are minimizing these problems.

Manufacturers warn users not to use printers in areas where there is an inordinate number of particles in the air. Foreign matter such as sawdust and paint spray can lodge in the ink outlet and clog the opening. The opening will clog, too, if the unit is not used often and the ink dries. Some printers have self-cleaning methods that flush the ink out of the opening when manual pressure is applied on the ink supply cartridge. High altitudes may also have an effect on the ink pressure.

On the plus side, ink jet printers, compared with dot matrix and letter quality, have fewer moving parts to wear out. The image is always the same intensity whereas ribbons used with impact printers tend to produce increasingly lighter images as they wear out, with the exception of single strike carbon ribbons. Ink jet printers are comparable in speed to dot matrix printers. Ink jet printing is more suitable for multicolor printing than ribbon based printers; it is easier to mix ink dots than multicolored ribbons for different color tones. As integrated software that combines word processing and color graphics becomes more popular, ink jet printers may receive greater consideration. Prices continue to tumble. They were very expensive only a few years ago; now low-cost ink jet printers are in the same price range as some dot matrix printers.

AMDEK's AMPLOT II has 6 pens. It can print text and graphics. A plotter generally is purchased for graphics output rather than for text alone.
Courtesy of AMDEK Corporation

Plotters

Plotters generally are used for graphic applications. Their resolution, or ability to draw fine detail, far exceeds that of most CRTs or printers. Plotters may draw text along with the graphic images, but are impractical as a device primarily devoted to text output. A plotter produces the images by controlling one or more pens, relative to an x-y coordinate system. Under software control the pens may move or draw freely across the drawing surface. This differs from most printers, which produce images in a top to bottom, line by line progression.

PAPERS

The most obvious items you need to make your printer behave admirably are the papers you use with it. Paper suppliers, in answer to user needs, have spawned myriad items to swell the growing printer products family.

Almost any form you could think of can be produced to run through the tractor feed of a printer—invoices, statements, labels, Rotary index cards in all sizes, tickets, checks. A catalog from a paper supply company will illustrate the wide choice available.

Forms, courtesy of Mesa Office Supply; photo, author

When you first begin looking for a printer, among the new terms you will run across are "Z" fold or "fanfold," or "continuous form" paper with the perforated tear-off edges. That ubiquitous item in every computer environment spits out connected sheets of paper along the tractor or pin feeder, over the top of the computer, and then drops them down behind the printer like unleashed floodwaters.

The normal 8½ x 11-inch plain paper originally packed in cartons of about 3,000 sheets is now available in lesser quantities of 1,000 sheets, and cleverly packaged by several companies.

Continuous form papers have grown to include a vast selection. There are letter and legal-size correspondence paper imprinted with your letterhead. If you don't like the appearance of the serrated edges, some manufacturers have developed clean tear edges; when the form feed paper sheets are separated, there is no evidence of a perforated edge. The same selection is available in carbon sets of two or three and also in carbonless multiprint forms.

Address labels come in different sizes: some three and four across a sheet, others in a single row. (Software determines how the addresses will print across the labels.)

Envelopes, plain and imprinted, are available with tear-off tractor feed edges, for the printer's paper feed mechanism.

Ledger paper, prepared with spreadsheet lines and in various widths and different rulings, is made in a variety of tints and color bar combinations. So are invoice and purchase order forms.

Continuous form checks and vouchers with your company's name can increase payroll department efficiency. Carbonless checks are provided with consecutive numbering, bank encoding information, bank account number, and bank branch codes imprinted in magnetic ink.

Quick forms exist that simulate telegrams but cost less. There is a dizzying variety to pick from, such as four- and six-part mailers with inserts, a four-part mailer with a single insert, a message and an outside envelope and a copy for your files. All have tear-off edges and require only that a customer's name be typed once.

There are continuous form Rolodex and index cards for fast reference. They are equally as convenient for typewriter use as for computers.

With such a selection, you may ask, "What isn't there?" So far . . . there's nothing available to tear off the perforated sides other than human hands.

Ribbons, Ribbon Cartridges, Ribbon Reinkers

After paper, the item your printer eats up fastest is ribbon. Printer ribbons are not standardized. They are unique to a printer and come in varied sizes and shapes. Printer ribbon replenishment availability and capability is an important consideration in the purchase of a printer.

Spool and cartridge ribbons for band, drum, chain, train, and matrix printers all differ. There are also multistrike and cloth ribbons, multicolor ribbons, and thermal ribbons. Some dot matrix printers use ordinary typewriter ribbons.

Printer ribbon cartridges are not standardized. They come in a variety of shapes for specific printers. Cartridges may be reloaded with fresh ribbon, or reinked; a procedure that will reduce ribbon replenishment by about 50 percent.
Courtesy of Aspen Ribbons, Inc.

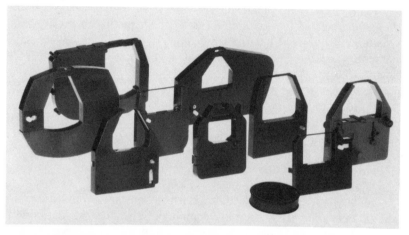

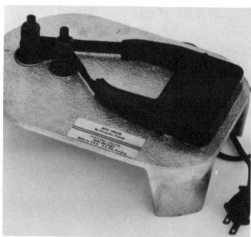

Ribbons can be reinked using the MacInker, a device on which you place used ribbon cartridges, and run them through the inked rollers of the unit. The ribbons are then ready for reuse.
Courtesy of Computer Friends

Cartridges that hold ribbons may be reloadable, so don't throw away the empty cartridge when the ribbon is used up or worn. There are companies that have created entire businesses based on reloading ribbons. There are also ribbon reinkers that sell for under $60 if you have ample need for one and are inclined to do it yourself.

Print Elements

An assortment of print elements for daisy wheel printers and thimbles for NEC Spinwriters can increase the variety of type fonts your letter quality printer can produce. Each element is available in different typefaces and in both plastic and metal. Metal reputedly lasts longer.

Fancy Printing

Among recent programs available are those that drive your printer to create unusual print fonts in a variety of sizes. There are packages with names such as FancyFont, and HexPrintR for dot matrix printers. They customize WordStar to support their capabilities. MagicPrint and MagicBind are used with a Diablo daisy wheel and a NEC Spinwriter printer. With some of these programs one can create columnar layouts, arrange the print around an illustration, and more. (See Chapter 14 for illustrations of what they can do.)

As you use your computer and printer to produce hard copy, you'll discover many ways to expand their capabilities. Life with a word processing system may be more versatile and easier than you may have ever dreamed.

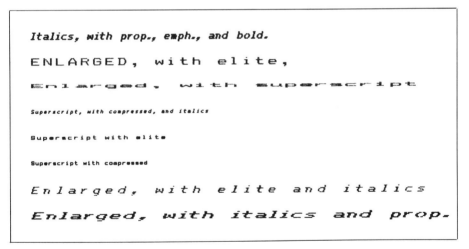

The output from a dot matrix printer can be varied tremendously. These are only a few of infinite combinations.

11. Optical Character Recognition Expands Word Processing

What may have been only a dream not so long ago becomes reality in the present and promise for the future when microchip technology is involved. Office equipment that integrates with computers is beginning to attract as much attention as computers themselves. Continuing research has spurred remarkable developments and new equipment. It infuses new life into existing technology and reduces the physical size and price of older systems.

One such dramatic size and price breakthrough is evident in optical character recognition units, or OCRs. Many of us are familiar with what OCRs do but may not know what they are called. Codes on bank checks and the printed bars and symbols on grocery products at the supermarket are read by optical character recognition units.

Optical character recognition is based on the idea that the special shape of each character printed on the medium can be identified by a photoelectric reading device. As the optical reader reads each character from the input medium, it translates the data into electrical impulses. These, in turn, are transmitted to the computer for processing and translating into binary codes of 1's and 0's, the form it can understand, and then retranslated as output in the form the user can understand.

What is the impact of such a product in the word processing environment? In nontechnical, time- and money-saving terms it means that a page of typewritten text can be fed directly into a computer's memory without a typist having to physically key the copy into the computer.

What happens instead? The operator feeds the typewritten page into the unit; the page is automatically read into the host computer's memory in anywhere from 15 to 25 seconds. The original sheet remains intact.

Three relatively low-priced and versatile units that merit attention are the Dest Workless Station (Dest Corporation) referred to as an "automatic document entry" system, the Multi-Font OCR Page Reader, TO-5000 (Totec Co., Ltd.), and the OMNI-READER (Oberon Int.). The units are designed to work with a range of compatible word processors in both the mini- and microcomputer environment. With new terminal emulator procedures that will load text from micros to minis to main frames and back again, any machine limitations will be easily overcome by applying ingenuity and creative transfer procedures.

This page of text would take 15 to 25 seconds to read and input to a computer with an OCR. It would take a fast typist 5 to 10 minutes to input the page using the keyboard. Dest estimates that a minimum of 70 pages can be copied per hour with 130–140 pages an hour typical. A fast typist, even at an unlikely nonstop top speed of 5 minutes per page, could input only 12 pages an hour.

Up to now, the lowest-priced OCRs were $15,000 and they were large and heavy. Prices for these new units begin under $10,000. OMNI-READER begins at $500. The machines require extra fonts to read more type styles, and necessary interfaces that will enter the specific word processor's codes into the file. All units are desktop size; the Dest measures 10 inches high, 16.5 inches wide, 21 inches deep, and weighs 36 pounds. The Totec measures under 12 inches high, 24 inches wide, 18 inches deep, and weighs 78 pounds. OMNI-READER is 15½ inches long, 3.2 inches wide, and weighs 2.6 pounds.

INCREASES PRODUCTION LOWERS COSTS

The obvious benefit and reasons for OCR are to speed word processing productivity. This alone could be worth the price as it affects convenience, morale, and money saved in many offices. But there is more to be gained from such a unit.

Documents roughly drafted on another word processor or a typewriter can be read into the office computer system so that dissimilar units' and word processors' output can "speak." What if an executive uses a portable computer to draft letters, contracts, or whatever, at home or on the road? His portable may be an entirely different operating system and disk size having no compatibility with the office unit. Rather than retyping the document for the office system, the hard copy is read by the OCR and, in seconds, it is converted and ready for editing or printing by office personnel.

Any incompatible (old and new) computer system can instantly become friendly and communicate; conversion problems are eliminated. Documents created on one system are quickly printed out, then read into the new system. Archived paper files can also be read into the word processing system and stored in disk memory for later retrieval.

The units can be the giant step a company requires to minimize paper files. Consider this scenario: You receive letters, reports, estimates from customers, another company, or an associate that you would like filed into your efficient computer storage instead of taking up physical file space. Almost any document can be loaded into the OCR, where it is copied onto disks and filed in the computer system for instant retrieval when necessary. The paper original can be discarded. If hard copy is required, a printout can be made.

OCR technology offers the potential to release personnel from time-consuming rote typing chores and make them available for greater productivity in other areas of an operation. Investment in an OCR system might result in a smaller investment in word processing equipment because units would not be tied up as long for many tasks. Any conventional typewriter would be, in essence, a word processing unit because the typed copy could be fed into the computer. Conceivably, the number of work stations in a multicomputer office could be reduced or those that exist could be used more efficiently. The number of word processor trained employees could be fewer. An OCR could be used throughout the integrated office, not only in the word processing center. It would have as much use in a professional office by a physician, lawyer, or architect as in any business.

With proper planning, an OCR system can yield a more productive work processing center and help to avoid rush projects, overtime work, and employee frustration.

HOW THE DEST SYSTEM WORKS

The Workless system is, literally, as easy to use as a photocopy machine. The only switches are on and off. There are few moving parts —enough to propel the page from the top tray, around the rollers, through the unit, and out to the bottom tray. As paper moves through the unit, it is read. The text may be displayed on the CRT or it may bypass the CRT and go directly to memory. When it goes directly to memory, the terminal can be used independently for other input. As many as 75 pages can be loaded for automatic feeding without an operator attending.

The basic unit reads copy using a "page image" system; no specific

The Dest Workless Station can accept up to 75 sheets at a time in its automatic sheet feeder with unattended operation. Each sheet enters the unit face up, goes in and around over rollers as it is read, and comes out at the bottom, face down.
Courtesy, Dest Corporation

formatting codes are read. Model 201, which lists at $6,995, can read a document prepared in the Courier 10 typeface and printed from IBM, Qume, Diablo, and Wang printers. It may be used with any minicomputer or microcomputer (with large enough memory) with which it can be interfaced via an RS232 cable. When the document must be reprinted it will require reformatting with the word processor codes.

A Model 202 that begins at $7,995 can read multitype styles. In addition to the standard Courier 10, a user may select up to 7 other type style recognition programs. Each additional type style is $495.

A high-speed, higher-priced Model 203 Turbofont will read at twice the speed of the other models, one page in less than 15 seconds and an estimated 250 pages per hour.

The OCR will read the document but it won't apply the codes of a specific word processing program to the file. Format options are available at $1,495 for popular word processing systems manufactured by Wang, IBM, NBI, CPT, and Xerox. Automatic page formatting capability includes paragraphs, tabs, indents, centers, underscores, columns, hyphens, end of page, and indexing of documents and job numbers where applicable.

When fitted with multiple font readers, Models 202 and 203 can also read different type styles and intermixed pitch settings on the same page without operator prompting

Red ink and pencil lines are invisible to the Workless Station. This means that a writer can indicate editing on an original but that editing will not interfere with the initial typed version. After the page is read into the computer, the typist can perform the necessary editing before the copy is returned to the writer. Can you imagine how that could save time for people in top management? For a president's speech? A manager's report? An interoffice letter? A physician's journal article? A professor's lecture?

Is the copy always perfectly read? The estimated error rate is less than one mistake in 10 typed pages or one in 300,000 characters. When a disfigured character is read, the Workless Station will make its best guess and highlight the character on the word processor for later checking and replacement by the operator.

What It Won't Do

Traditionally, OCRs required special paper, line spacing, character marking, operator control, and other preset parameters. All that has been changed and revolutionized. Yet a few limitations exist.

The Workless Station won't read hand lettering or any written editing. It won't read logos and letterheads containing graphics and typefaces with which it is not familiar. It will read only prescribed type fonts for which it has been fitted. The base unit accepts one 10-pitch type font. Among the additional fonts available are the more popular styles such as Prestige Elite, Letter Gothic, and Courier 72, all in 10/12 pitch and others. The more type font flexibility you desire, the more the unit will cost. There are 8 type fonts available.

It won't read type that is printed on onionskin paper or cardboard stock; it must be paper that will feed through the roller system. However, almost any type of paper can be read, including photocopied and colored sheets. It will have difficulty reading copy that has been marked over with anything but red ink. It won't read type placed along the length of the sheet; the text must be on letter or legal-size paper and printed horizontally.

TOTEC MULTI-FONT OCR

Totec's TO-5000 OCR offers features similar to the Dest Workless Station Model 203. A significant difference is that the TO-5000 copies via a straight paper path rather than rollers that move the paper around and over. Therefore the weight of paper it can read is greater and may be anything from onionskin to heavy paper. Totec's estimated reading speed is about 15 seconds a page which also compares to Dest's Model 203 Turbofont unit and is in the same $9,995 price range equipped with a single font. Extra fonts are $495. The TO-5000 is complete with interfaces for popular word processor formats.

The TO-5000 can read letterheads and some graphics. It is compatible with most word processing programs used on minis and micros and the interfaces are included in the price.

For anyone whose business requirements will benefit from an OCR, write to the companies for their brochures and for names of local sales representatives. Watch ads in business and computer magazines for systems advertised by other companies.

The TO-5000 Multi-Font OCR Page Reader from Totec Company, Ltd., has a straight paper path. The hopper will hold 30 sheets at a time and process them without operator attention. Text can be sent via an autodialer to a printer and private communication lines, to a word processor, or to a host computer system.
Courtesy, Totec Company, Ltd.

OMNI-READER IS A BREAKTHROUGH

The OMNI-READER represents an industry breakthrough in price and technology. The unit is designed to interface with microcomputers using the standard RS 232 connection. Instead of a sheet of paper being processed through a machine as in the Dest and Totec, the user scans the page using a tracking guide with a head that reads the document. In addition to the fonts that are designed to be read by the system, the unit will "learn" a new type style even if it hasn't been previously programmed in.

The low-priced OMNI-READER operates simply: a printed or typed page is placed under the ruler and aligned on a special tablet. The desired information is scanned by the read head and input into the computer where it can be edited.
Courtesy of Oberon International

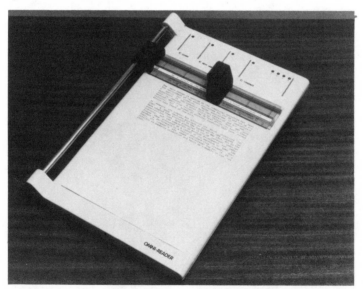

COMPANIES

☐ THE WORKLESS STATION

Dest Corporation
2380 Bering Dr.
San Jose, CA 95131
1-800-538-7582

☐ TO-5000 MULTI-FONT OCR

Totec Co. Ltd.
19151 Parthenia St., Ste. A
Northridge, CA 91324
(213) 993-9413

☐ OMNI-READER

Oberon International
5525 MacArthur Blvd.
Irving, TX 75062
(214) 252-8453
and
47 Romney St.
London SW, England
44 1 222-0518

12. "Dedicating" Keys to Software Commands

Dedicated word processing machines have the standard typing keyboard enhanced with one or two rows of extra keys across the top. Each key is labeled with its own special funciton: move a block of type, save a document, find a document, etc.

On a microcomputer each conventional letter on the keyboard, when combined with a control key and another keyboard character, performs a task that the dedicated machine assigns to a single key. The ability to change the tasks of these keys with different programs is one of the reasons microcomputers are so popular . . . and versatile.

But people argue: Which is best? Which is fastest? Companies that sell dedicated machines maintain that their units are easier to learn, more efficient. Yet micros are winning the race in the marketplace; lower price and more capabilities are a hard combination to fight. People are willing to work harder, stretch their learning potential, and exercise finger dexterity to perform manipulations with multiple keys.

The inevitable is happening. Mini manufacturers are offering computers that will accept more programs and become less dedicated (some even moved into the micro market). Micro manufacturers and software distributors are offering ways to make their machines emulate dedicated processors.

Ever the twain shall meet in this crazy world of high technology that makes liars out of adages.

The result? Macros.

A "macro" or a "macro instruction" is a series of keystrokes that could be characters, functions, or both, and that can be remembered and used by a program to perform a specific operation. A macro within a program can alter the character and the number of characters that can be assigned to a single key.

With a macro you can write seemingly endless thoughts that appear almost magically with the stroke of a SINGLE KEY! To make matters more interesting, some macros have been used so ingeniously that an entire microcomputer keyboard could be altered so that *every key* could become dedicated to another purpose, not only those already used as function keys. Even function keys can be assigned new roles. And each key could be given a different role for each program used. That's more than any dedicated machine could offer!

What does that mean in the overall picture? If you don't appreciate hitting two, three, or four keys to accomplish a specific function, you can exercise control over your keyboard's response. Some keyboards already have 10 to 15 "function" keys that software writers utilize. But that is so few when a program may require 50 or more commands.

With a macro it is possible to:

1. Literally change the keyboard and customize beyond your wildest dreams (depending upon how wild your dreams are).
2. Make these changes so they are the same or different for any program you use.
3. Change the number keys on the keypad so that each becomes a text input command.
4. Change keys even while another program is running and define a key for a new function.
5. Store the definitions for use every time the program is invoked, or be able to change them whenever you like.
6. Make a single key become a different number of characters from one to perhaps an entire page.

It's all done with the software. Several word processing programs include macros with instructions for using them. A program may already have a key titled "macro definition." Hit that key and the keystrokes that follow will be stored in a file when the macro definition key is hit again. When you want to use that series of keystrokes, use the "invoke" macro key and all information defined on the key will appear.

Assume you wanted one key to contain the closing for correspondence: "Sincerely yours, four character returns and your name." You would assign all the necessary keystrokes to the one definition. When you want to place the closing at the end of the letter, you hit only the "invoke macro key" and it's all there. One keystroke for about 25 keystrokes. Nice.

Several programs exist that provide a macro capability to other software. Some are for specific machines. Some can be used for many machines depending upon the operating system and installation capabilities of the program. Integrated software that moves data between several modules uses macros to simplify the strokes needed to accomplish these moves.

HOW DO THE PROGRAMS WORK?

Essentially, each program is a software "utility" that sits in the computer's memory and is completely invisible to other programs. It's like Aladdin. Ask him to rub his magic lamp and when you want any single key to change its role so that it represents a string of information, you send the message and *pouf!* it happens, and it is there when you need it. Change your mind? Another message and *pouf!* it is gone.

Assume, for example, that you're using Perfect Writer, a word processing program that requires placing repetitive commands such as @BEGIN(TEXT) and @END(TEXT) before and after several blocks of copy in a document. @BEGIN(TEXT) requires 13 keystrokes. Assign that command to the 1 key on the numerical keypad. Type 1 and watch as the program inputs @BEGIN(TEXT) with a single key.

When you use the PIP or Copy commands of your operating system, the command PIP A: = B:, which you type many times, requires the following 12 keystrokes:

shift
P
I
P
space
SHIFT A
SHIFT :
=
SHIFT
B
SHIFT :
<CR>

Can you estimate the time saved and potential errors eliminated if the entire command resided on one key? Assign it to the ¯ tilde, for example, so that when you strike ¯, the output will be:

PIP A: = B:

But that's only the tip of the iceberg.

You can assign entire paragraphs to one key. Imagine preparing a letter of inquiry that always has the salutation and first paragraph the same. They're all input with a single keystroke. Next add your personalized paragraph. Then with another keystroke the final paragraph and complimentary close will be input. It's another method for making boilerplate, or form, paragraphs, similar to those used with boilerplate letters in a merge program. But many form letters are not candidates for merge printings. The macros serve the purpose and can be ever ready for a single letter or several letters. In the following you would type only the date and the client's name and specific information. Sections 1 and 2 would each be stored in a macro definition file and require a single keystroke to bring them on screen into a document file.

---

date

Ms. Alida Hayes
1234 Main St
Anywhere US 90222

Dear Ms. Hayes:

1. It gives me great pleasure to inform you that you have won a free trip to

   (You could personalize the message for a specific client in this space. Perhaps add the conditions, times, and any other details for this particular person's trip. Then hit another SINGLE KEY with the following text assigned to it:)

2. We appreciate the opportunity of working with you for these travel arrangements. Please call this office between the hours of 9 and 5 to verify your acceptance. We are here to answer your questions and to help to make your travel an exciting experience.

   Sincerely yours,

   Donald Domore
   Vice President
   Free Travel Co.

Some programs have more power than others, just as some genies do. When you evaluate a program, look for one that will do what you think you want it to do . . . or more. Anyone who makes one wish and has it fulfilled undoubtedly will have greater wishes in the future.

WHY CHANGE THE KEYBOARD?

The key arrangement for commands established by programmers for various software packages does not necessarily match the logic of the person using that software. This applies to programs other than word processing, too—spreadsheets, inventories, file programs, data base programs.

Consider that the computer's keyboard is based on the old typewriter QWERTY keyboard with its illogical placement of letters. The QWERTY keyboard resulted when Christopher Latham Sholes actually sought an *inefficient* key placement for his invention. Typists typed faster than the machine would go. So Mr. Sholes arranged the keys to make it *harder* for them to type efficiently and purposely slow them up.

The more logical Dvorak keyboard, proposed by August Dvorak in the early 1930s, has a more practical key arrangement so that characters used most often are located where fingers find them most readily. Vowels are on the left and consonants at the right. In almost every typing speed contest, people who use the Dvorak keyboard outspeed those on the QWERTY keyboard considerably, sometimes as much as twice as fast and more than 200 words a minute. Typing 100 words a minute is considered very fast on a QWERTY.

But if changing a whole keyboard seems too drastic, with macros you can assign functions you want where you want them.

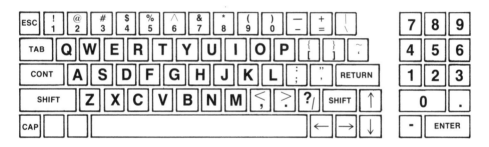

The key placement of the QWERTY keyboard has become standard in the industry.

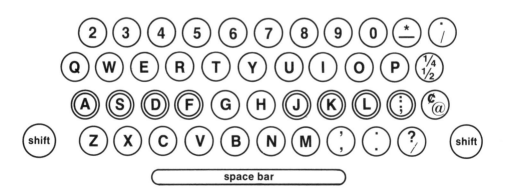

Placement of the keys on the Dvorak keyboard, proposed by August Dvorak in the 1930s, has a more logical arrangement than the QWERTY.

WHICH PROGRAMS ACCOMPLISH THESE FEATS?

The available programs that can accomplish key changes are capable of doing much more. They are more like small processors within a program; they could be defined as a single instruction that invokes a series of additional instructions. Each varies in one or more of its capabilities, how it works, and in the nuances it can accomplish. Note that some are only for PCDOS and MSDOS and others are for CP/M, but this can change.

Key-Fixer

For the IBM PC, IBM XT, and selected PC compatible units. Will work with most popular programs for customizing keys to specific commands and strings. Vertex Systems, 7950 W. Fourth St., Los Angeles, CA 90048. $69.95

K-Key

A program specifically for defining keys on the Kaypro computer. It also has the capability of shutting off the disk drive and screen controls, the keyboard click, and more. It's compatible with all programs. K-Key is a product of Puck, Inc., 526 E. Smith St., Kent, WA 98031. $29.95

ManyKey

An Osborne computer program that will store function-key definitions for different .COM file programs. From CompuMagic Inc., P.O. Box 780, Severn, MD 21144. $20

ProKey

Compatible with PCDOS and MSDOS systems. The program, with its customized definitions, is loaded into the PC RAM at boot-up and remains resident under almost any other program that follows. ProKey is from RoseSoft, 4710 University Way N.E., Seattle, WA 98105. $75

SMARTKEY II

For CP/M and PCDOS and MSDOS systems. With it a user can redefine the function of any or all keys as a single character, line, paragraph, even a whole page. It can be used within a program while a file is being created or edited. From Heritage Software, Inc., 2130 A. Vermont Ave., Los Angeles, CA 90007. $89

WS-Keys

Designed to work with WordStar on CP/M and MSDOS systems. It addresses only the 10 function keys so that you can arrange them in a more comfortable sequence with a maximum of 6 characters. You can assign different commands to the function keys from those that are offered by default with WordStar. WS-Keys is considered an "extra" for its major offer on the disk: a program to access many print capabilities of WordStar needed for different dot matrix printers. WS-KEYS is from CMB3 Enterprises, Walnut Creek, CA 94598. $49.95

FEATURES TO LOOK FOR

A comparison chart would not be valid since each program works differently as it applies to different operating systems. The following features are offered so you will know what to look for. Check them against any stand alone macro program. Also check them for the macros offered in a specific word processing program. Some of the questions are culled from a chart offered by RoseSoft, distributors of ProKey.

Is the program compatible with your hardware?
Number of keys that can be defined?
Maximum length of a string?
Can the strings be edited?
Can the strings contain "fill in the blank" fields?
Can strings be created while you are actually using the program?
Can strings make references to other strings?
Can strings be saved in standard ASCII files?
Can files of strings be merged with one another?
Can keyboard layouts be modified with keyboard diagrams?
Is there a file for creating a Dvorak or other keyboard?
Can a key be redefined without losing original definitions of other keys?
What software will it work with that you use? Or plan to use?
Does it have predefined strings for WordStar? SuperCalc?
    VisiCalc? dBase II, etc?
Is there an interacter on-screen tutorial?
Is the manual adequate? Indexed? Is there an example?
What is the most recent version?
How are updates provided?

13. Word Processing Training— What, How, When, Who?

ord processing has gained a reputation of being "hard to learn." The person contemplating the switch from typewriter to the commands of a word processor program is dealing with a great unknown and something new—two conditions that throw many people into a dither. It could be only a matter of mental attitude. How hard is it to learn to drive a car? Use a camera? Become familiar with how a microwave oven works?

Word processing programs are filled with a series of complex commands that enable one to accomplish many objectives. These commands pose the same challenges as those in any other "new" subject. Once you delve into and tackle the problems, the unfamiliar becomes well worn and habitual. The user is off and running. And excited. If there are people who have learned word processing and still opt for a typewriter, I haven't met them.

Software developers kill themselves trying to make commands of a program "user friendly." But be suspect of programs advertised as "easy to learn in only 30 minutes." A program that is so easy may lack important text manipulation capabilities.

Carefully investigate what any program will and will *not* do. WordStar is reputedly hard to learn; yet it has not stopped hundreds of thousands of people from learning it.

Manuals for many programs are well designed graphically with fewer pages and more white space so the program's commands appear less awesome. By oversimplification, presenting only the commands needed for a beginner, the manual may omit procedures that are important once the user is past the basics. In addition to manuals, documentation may also include paste-on labels for the keys, reference cards, and keyboard overlays, all of which are a definite help.

How can you investigate a program before you buy it? And once you buy it, how can you learn it quickly and apply its features to your needs?

TYPES OF TRAINING AIDS

Training aids for many popular software packages have spawned an entire new industry ranging from 60-second demo disks to full semesters of classes.

Demo Disks

Software vendors have taken advantage of demo disks and they may be your first introduction to a software package in a dealer's showroom.

A demo, short for demonstration disk, is usually an overview of a program that shows the user the basics. This quick synopsis may run anywhere from a few minutes to a fifteen-minute demonstration. The short demo may present the features for the viewer to watch on screen, moving from one frame to the next by itself. Longer demos may be "user interactive," which means that you actually fill in answers the program requires.

Demo disks are a boon to dealers and salespeople as well as the customer. They save the salesperson's time by showing you the program. They give you the opportunity to go through the menus and the concepts of the program at your own pace and as often as you need to get the feel of how the program proceeds.

It stands to reason that such disks present only the essential aspects of a program. They require the correct input before they proceed to the next step. If you do something wrong there is usually a beep, but no explanation of how you erred. After you are familiar with a program for an interactive demo, ask the dealer for an in-depth presentation from a working disk.

Manuals and On-Disk Tutorials

Every program comes with a manual; fortunately competition has forced a tremendous improvement in their quality. Some companies provide a lesson plan in the manual that you follow using the program.

Often, there are accompanying tutorials on a lesson disk; these should be more thorough than a demonstration disk. You should be able to repeat any step that is not clear, back up to a previous lesson, or select a lesson in any order. Some training disks, like demo disks, only accept the correct answer without explaining if the wrong answer is entered. They do not allow you to go back one or two steps or to zero in on any portion of a lesson without plowing through the entire lesson again.

Generally, on-disk tutorials provided with a specific program are

A tutorial on a disk is included with MicroPro's software. A keyboard tour is one of the first lessons in the series called FEARNOT. The user follows the directives at the bottom right of the screen.
Courtesy of MicroPro International Corporation

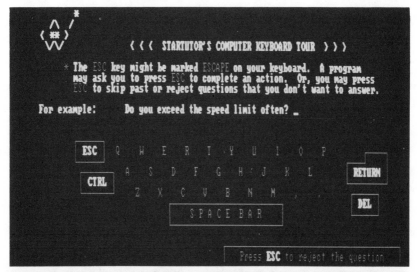

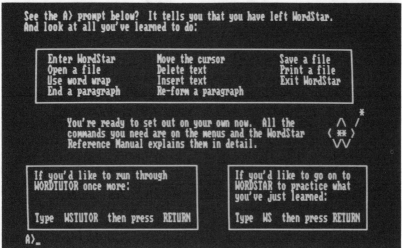

WordTutor is an on-disk lesson for the WordStar word processing program. It follows the educational dictum to summarize what has been learned in this final screen of the lesson.
Courtesy of MicroPro International Corporation

A lesson on screen for the program Lotus 1-2-3, an integrated software program that includes word processing, appears with instructions to the user in the ATI Training Power series.
Courtesy of American Training International, Inc.

beneficial, especially for the beginner. The lessons are designed to be used with that program and that version of the program and on the computer system for which it was ordered. In an office where new personnel must be introduced to a program frequently, such self-learning tutorials can be worthwhile.

Outside companies have seen the opportunity for marketing supplemental tutorials on disk (other than those provided with a specific program). A variety of stand alone training programs are available for different operating systems but often they must be installed for the user's specific terminal. One problem is that they become outdated when a program is revised and the resulting differences can cause problems for neophytes.

Sometimes subtle differences in some computer systems will prevent the programs from running as advertised on "all" compatible systems. They may also require more RAM memory than you might expect . . . so be sure to investigate the requirements before you purchase a supplemental training guide.

Another caution. A company may update and issue a new version of the word processing program but neglect to update the manual or the on-screen tutorial. How do you know? Check the version of the program offered and compare it with the version number on the documentation. If the program is a later version than the documentation be sure there are supplemental instructions for the update.

Guidebooks, Tape Cassettes, Videocassettes

As the industry matures and sees a potential market for a product, it strives to fill that market. The publishing industry is working hard to provide guidebooks to many programs where the original documentation falls short. Many of these books are excellent and some are no better than the manuals. Watch for book reviews and ask for recommendations from other users.

Instructions on tape cassettes that are used with a tape recorder may be a good investment, especially when the same program is used on different types of machines in an office. The tape is "machine independent," as opposed to a disk, which must be ordered for the specific system. A tape explaining WordStar, for example, could be used with a machine that has 5¼- or 8-inch disks, CP/M, Apple, or an IBM PC operating system. Tapes also permit a user to go back and review any portion of a lesson. The drawback? Not every machine supports every feature of a program. An example would be an explanation of a "highlighted" menu but a particular terminal may not have highlighting.

Videocassettes and interactive videodisks provide visual and audio support. They are ideal for classroom introduction to a program and a general overview.

Keyboard Helps—Reference Cards

More software companies are supplying stick-on tabs for key fronts or tops so you will know which key moves the cursor in what direction, scrolls, performs block moves, etc. The problem with these is that the stick-on tabs apply to the word processing program and that same key may have a different function in another type of program.

Another device is a keyboard overlay dedicated to one program only. When you change programs you change the overlay. There are overlays, often called templates, that give an entire reference list of commands for a specific program.

Watch for a dizzying variety of reference cards, flip-back spiral-bound books, and other formats with the prompts for a specific program printed so they are idiotically easy to find.

Classes and "People" Training

On a grander scale, there are classes offered by individuals, adult educational programs of local high schools and colleges, computer societies, computer vendors, users' groups, and a proliferating number of computer schools.

In an office environment employees may learn more quickly from personal contact with a teacher in a one to one situation or in a classroom environment than trying to figure out a program alone. This may be instead of, or in addition to, the training aids already described. When planning a training program for personnel, certain questions must be addressed.

1. Who will operate the computer? How will training be offered?
2. Who will provide the training?
3. How will the employee be motivated to learn?
4. How can the effectiveness of the training be evaluated?

Whether present or potential employees are familiar with word processing or have no exposure to the principles of computers, training will be required. The amount of time needed per employee will vary; so will the costs, according to how the needs are met.

TEMPORARY HELP

Temporary employment agencies offer training programs. As the demand for trained help grows, some of the leading temporary employment agencies are starting their own classes. They know that employers, faced with sick leave, turnover, and peak load understaffing, appreciate available help who can fill in quickly. A temporary employee, trained in the way a variety of different systems work, may be requested as a trainer. It's a potentially powerful way to draw in personnel when needed.

HOW EFFECTIVE IS TRAINING?

Word processing is a comparative newcomer in many offices and it takes time and check lists to evaluate how well it is working. A reevaluation of how efficiently word processing has been implemented in an office may be warranted if any of the following situations appear:

☐ **Slow turnaround time.** Four hours is a good standard for letters and short documents. Any longer turnaround time should be investigated.

☐ **Chronic complaints and excuses.** Do users repeatedly complain about conditions? Give excuses for not completing work? List these complaints, how often voiced, and by whom. Steps may be needed to change personnel, training, environment, and/or procedures.

☐ **Users bypass.** Any time users go out of their way to avoid working with the system, you have a problem.

☐ **Low morale/high turnover.** Are there too many rules? Restrictions? Is the worker isolated? Is the pay adequate?

☐ **Poor control; retrieval problems.** Does the word processing staff have difficulty finding previously recorded material? Do they consistently use the wrong version of a frequently revised document? Look at the methods for organizing disk, files, cataloging procedures. Their use should be part of the training.

☐ **Too much paperwork.** Computers are supposed to reduce paperwork, not add to it. But some companies try so hard to expedite work that they create more forms to fill out just to move work through the word processing department. Establish effective channels and be ready to change any that don't work.

There is no one, or best, answer as to how word processing training can be learned or should be taught in your specific situation and at any one time with any one employee. There is every probability that you will try one or all the above methods at various times. Problems should be defined and redefined in terms of your own equipment, personnel, and expectations. Knowing the climate for problems that can occur and how to cope with them will help generate practical decisions based on wise predictions.

COMPANIES AND PROGRAMS

The following companies provide disks, tape, and video learning aids. Books, pamphlets, spiral reference cards will be found in bookstores and in computer stores.

☐ **MICROPRO TRAINING GUIDES**

MicroPro International Corp.
33 San Pablo Ave.
San Rafael, CA 94903
(415) 499-1200

Disks/videocassette tapes.

☐ **ATI TRAINING POWER**

American Training International
3800 Highland Ave.
Manhattan Beach, CA 90260
(213) 546-4735

Disks/manuals.

☐ **CDEX PERSONAL COMPUTER TRAINING LIBRARY**

CDEX Corporation
5060 El Camino Real
Los Altos, CA 94022
(415) 964-7600

Disks/manuals.

☐ **FLIPTRACK**

FlipTrack Learning Systems
526 N. Main St., Box 771
Glen Ellyn, IL 60137
(312) 790-1117

Tape cassettes.
Manual.

14. Creative Graphics and Font Fun with a Word Processor

ord processor programs are designed to work with letters and numbers. Not pictures. Right? Wrong. Applying some creativity and imagination can turn your word processor into a "graphics" terminal—with limitations of course. We're not suggesting that you can create Disney-like animation or even business charts that will inspire megabuck contracts. There are high-powered graphics programs for that purpose and many that can be integrated with a word processing program. For any sizable graphic needs, investigate art and presentation graphics software or systems specifically designed with text and paint features such as The Macintosh.

We are suggesting that simple illustrations, word logos, and varied appearances in typeface sizes and styles can be achieved with a word processor. A dot matrix printer can expand that potential further. Even a letter quality printer has graphics capability if you give it a little extra attention.

When, why, and how would you have use for such shenanigans?

Consider the computer store that wants to keep costs down, yet invites customers to a first anniversary "salebration." Management refused to spend 4 cents each for printed letterheads and used plain fanfold paper at ½ cent each. The mailing was sent with no letterhead, no imprint. The type was ordinary dot matrix using a faded blue ribbon. Theoretically, the letter was individualized, but it was too obviously generated by a mail merge program with each of the 500 names inserted into a letter.

"Deadly," "uninspired" describe the invitation kindly. Given the sophistication of mail pieces that come across everyone's desk daily, to think such a letter would gain any serious attention was naïve. Worse still was that it presented a poor image of the store.

How could that same letter have been presented with more pizzazz, more oomph, and not add to the cost? How could simple graphics be generated using either a dot matrix or letter quality printer, and a basic word processing program?

By applying a little originality and creativity.

Imagine that you were to do a mailing and wanted something more ingenious than your name and address in ordinary typewriter type. What could you do?

USE ALPHANUMERICS AS DESIGN ELEMENTS

Each character of the alphabet, the numbers and other symbols on a typewriter keyboard, are individual design elements capable of uses far beyond spinning them into words and balance sheets. Graphics designers have been using these elements creatively for countless centuries. (Remember the illustrated manuscripts painted painstakingly by monks before the printing press was invented?) If you have a dot matrix printer, and a program that will produce different type fonts, you can, for example, create a wild assortment of graphics for a letterhead and use it for envelopes, business cards, and every kind of correspondence. Keep the design in a file called LETHEAD.FRM (letterhead form) and each time you need it, insert it at the top of the new file and you're ready to go with customized stationery.

It could be a form as simple as:

JANE ADAMS   12345 FRONTON ST

ANYTOWN US 12204

(619) 756 0973

Observe that the name is bold face and the address is spaced to become a block of type.

Here's another idea:

___ **JANE J. ADAMS** | CONSULTANT
    ___ 12345 fronton st | to the
      ___ anytown us 12204 | COMPUTER
       ___ (619) 756 0973 | INDUSTRY

Perhaps you can create a logo using your initial or the name of your company.

J J A
Jane J Adams   C O N S U L T A N T

Another idea? Use a standard symbol to suggest and represent a visual image such as:

~~~~~~~~~
W F
WAVE of the FUTURE Software
                12345 fronton st
                ANYTOWN US 12204
                (619) 756 0973

~~~~
DEAR SIR:

It is possible to preprint the letterhead on a package of fanfold paper, then refold it and use the paper for your correspondence. Just like having printed letterheads. You may also experiment with a 12 or 14 pitch print for the letterhead, then a 10 pitch for the correspondence. It won't look quite so "typed" throughout. (See page 162.)

STORING DESIGN SHAPES FOR READY USE

Another writing project might call for a repeat shape within a document, perhaps a rectangle or square, for a specific illustration. It's pointless to draw the boxes each time you need them, so create and store the shape in a file for ready insertion. A recent newsletter project required boxed spaces in which illustrations would be pasted later. Normally, blank space would be left, the illustrations pasted, and then an artist would draw an inked line around them.

Boxes were created and stored as a file ready for use in the correct size required. Typed lines served the same function as the inked lines. Double printing or boldface rendered the lines as dark as those that were inked and they reproduced satisfactorily in the final photographic print process.

The rectangles below are stored in a file named RECT25X3.1NS (Rectangle 25 columns by 3 lines.Insert.) A larger rectangle of 15 columns by 6 lines is stored in another file so it can be read into a document as needed. It is possible to perform a poor man's idea of "imaging" by adding or subtracting characters vertically or horizontally to change the shape.

The lines could be closer together and the shape slightly smaller by requesting they be printed at a different "pitch" (see Pitch discussion, page 162).

You can add a message within those shapes, too.

```
-------------------------
If you are careful you can also create a box and a  |  ** EXTRA **    |
column. The care required depends upon the software |       JOB       |
and how the paragraphs readjust when you reform.    |     NEEDED      |
You could easily lose the whole thing as one giant  |       FOR       |
paragraph with lines and text all mashed together as|    TEENAGER     |
one. The trick is to create the block as you type. With |              |
most programs, you can't go back and add it at the  |                 |
side; you have to type it in line by line as you write |               |
the text. It takes time, but it is a challenge once you |               |
get the idea. For creating newsletters or flyers, the |                |
potential is there.                                 -------------------------
```

If you plan to do much of this, select a word processing program that has the capability of moving blocks of text by columns. Not all programs can. Column block moves increase versatility and page design tremendously. A few word processing programs can do minimal line drawing. When coupled with a program that additionally can instruct the printer to create different font output, the options are infinite.

To speed up the procedure create some of these special effects at the end of the document in which you plan to use it, or in another file. When you are satisifed, assemble the parts or bring each "designed" shape into the document where it belongs. Remember! Retain a copy at the end of the file or in another file. Should you accidentally reformat the section you could destroy the entire effect. A backup will save time.

PRINT SOFTWARE TO CHANGE TEXT APPEARANCE

There are print programs that will produce column print capability for selected printers, along with true proportional spacing whether the type is justified or unjustified. (See the example produced by MagicPrint on page 167.) Their own manual uses a simple graphic:

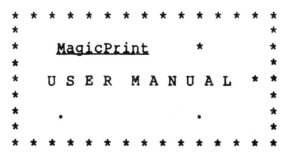

Several programs on the market will customize word processing software to bring out the capabilities of a dot matrix printer. A character set can be condensed, compressed, changed to double width, pica and elite, italics, and more. It is also possible to mix block graphics and regular printing. HexPrintR from C.I. Software, the FancyFont System from SoftCraft, SoftStyle from Softstyle, Inc. Watch advertisements for additional programs that will customize your specific word processor and dot matrix printer and be sure it works with the computer and disk operating system you are using.

Certainly, the trend to integrated business graphics and word processing is an advantage. Word processing, graphics, a data base, communications link, and scheduling all in one package require certain systems and memory size. Not everyone needs all the tools in an integrated business package nor may he or she require that the data be generated automatically. (A spreadsheet program such as SuperCalc, recommended for creating text charts, can generate simple bar charts based on the information given in the spreadsheet.)

Changing "Pitch" and Line Height of the Type Characters

A few programs permit you to alter the pitch or the number of characters per inch within a document. This feature enables you to space the letters differently, closer together or farther apart. Mixing them in one document can heighten visual interest and impact. Even if it's for a bill!

The number of lines per inch may also be varied. Line height is the height of one line of type measured by the number of lines per inch.

Changing the Type Font on a Wheel Type Printer

A dot matrix printer is infinitely more versatile for producing different print appearances. But what about a printer with daisy wheel or thimble element? Many letter quality printers have from 9 to as many as 20 types of fonts available by changing the print element.

The word processing program can make wheel changing easier if it has a print pause command that says, essentially, "Stop the printer during this run and let the user change the element." If a program does not have such a command, you will have to improvise; either type the entire document with a different element or stand by the printer and stop it at the necessary place in the document, change the element, and then continue. Often it's easier to stop the printer manually at the exact place you wish the print to be changed than it is to halt the program. Why? Because most printers have a buffer that permits the text to continue beyond the point where you asked the program to stop typing. To stop a printer manually, use a pause button or lift any part of the printer that causes a pause.

This type font was altered by changing the Courier font print element to another called TECHMATH/TIMES ROMAN. Some of its characters would not be appropriate for document typing, although others would be delightful. The semicolon, for example, would only produce the Greek symbol for micro: μ. The quote mark produces the symbol pi, as π. So one has to be careful and study the printout of the element selected. Here is the complete character font of that type element. After it is printed, another pause is required to change the element back to the Courier element.

abcdefghijklmnopqrstuvwxyz   1234567890− =[ ]μ',./Ω
ABCDEFGHIJKLMNOPQRSTUVWXYZ
! #∫% β*( )＿+{ } :π<>?|

Here are ideas for using different type fonts:

Consider creating letterheads using an Old English type thimble on the NEC Spinwriter or a daisy wheel printer. Run a block of fanfolded paper, or individual stationery, through your printer and have it ready for reprinting when you have correspondence to go.

Request that some sections print as 12 pitch, some as 10 pitch for variety and emphasis to visually change the appearance. Consider printing twice on the same sheet of paper using two different files, thus altering the image of the output. Carefully "register" the placement of the print on the second file so it doesn't overprint the first output.

Producing graphics requires experimentation, but the results are worth the effort. You'll exercise creativity and better appreciate the potential of graphics as an attention getter.

Examples of graphics created on the screen and printed with a letter quality printer follow. The hot air balloon is from the on-screen example showing how the program, StarIndex by MicroPro, is used.

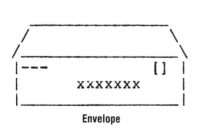

Envelope

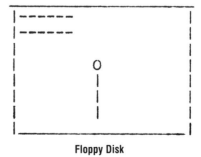

Floppy Disk

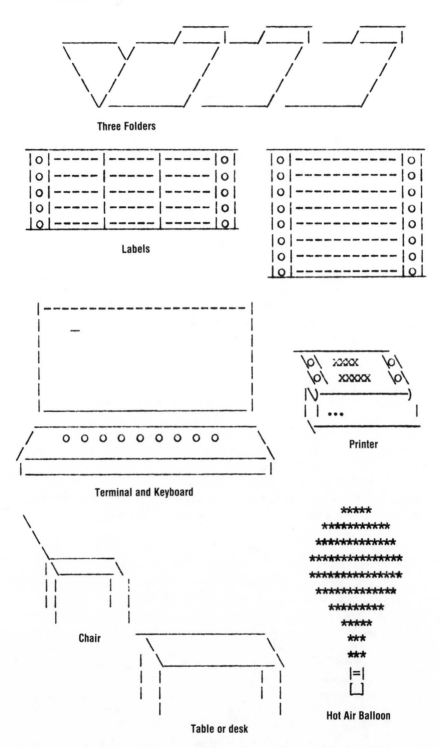

Three Folders

Labels

Terminal and Keyboard

Printer

Chair

Table or desk

Hot Air Balloon

Examples of Printing Output

Various dot matrix printers and plotters will produce different results. Often the software must be "installed" to utilize the features of a printer. Conversely, some printers cannot take advantage of the software capabilities.

x x x x x x x x x x x x x x x x x x x x x x x x x x x x x x x x x x x

WORDSTAR INSTALLED FOR THE C. ITOH PROWRITER PRINTER

This line is in PICA (10 CPI) style type. It is the fastest type
    face and pitch, and is very useful for listings.

This line is in ELITE (12 CPI) style type. This is a good type for letters.

This line is in the unusual PROPORTIONAL type face. NOTICE that each letter has a different width.
  This type face also allows M I C R O S P A C I N G.   !!!!!!!!!!!!!!!!!
  Unfortunately WordStar does not support right margin justification with this type face on this printer.

This line is in COMPRESSED print. This allows you to put a lot on one line. This type face is also good for listings.

Double width printing may be applied to:
    COMPRESSED, PROPORTIONAL, ELITE, and PICA.

This printer also has a   GREEK   character set: αβγδεξηθικ....
                  and a GRAPHICS character set: ⊢⊣●□◆♥♦♣....
                  (for this to print correctly, SW 2-6 must be closed)

WordStar installed for the C. Itoh Printer by C. I. Software.
Courtesy of C. I. Software

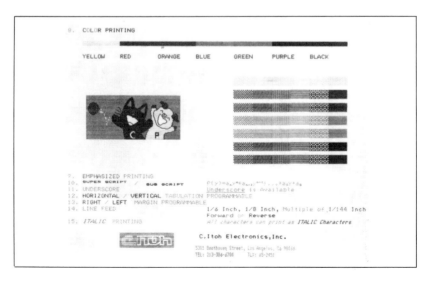

A C. Itoh color printer can produce pure color and color mixtures for both print and illustrations.
Courtesy of C. Itoh Electronics, Inc.

```
This line is in NORMAL PICA (10 CPI) character pitch.

This line is in ELITE (12 cpi) pitch.

The unusual PROPORTIONAL type face does NOT have a fixed pitch.

This line is in CONDENSED pitch. This allows you to put lots of information in the space of a single printed line.

If you have the need to put as much information as possible on a page, try using the condensed type pitch and the
EPSON superscripts with 7/72" line spacing. It packs information into an increasibly small space!

Double width printing may be applied to:
NORMAL, ELITE, PROPORTIONAL and CONDENSED.

This printer also has ITALICIZED type face printing.

         Your Epson can generate EMPHASIZED,

             or DOUBLE DENSITY,

          or BOTH OF THEM TOGETHER.


    WordStar can highlight with DOUBLE STRIKE,

         or with BOLDFACE (3 strikes),

     or with BOTH OF THEM TOGETHER (6 strikes).
```

WordStar installed for the Epson FX printer.
Courtesy of C. I. Software

```
.g53                                        HOW TO USE THE KEYBOARD
.*t
HOW TO USE THE KEYBOARD
                                                              4.5 Operator Aids
.c
4.5 Operator Aids                          ----------------------------------------------------------------
)                                          PURPOSE:  To provide an operator with a means of performing specific functions by
.#b                                                  pressing a single key.
                                           ----------------------------------------------------------------
ACME Computer Manual
.blc                                       Item        Field             Operator            System
4-#                                        No.         Description       Action              Response
.blr
08/20/84                                   1    Function key F1.         Press F1 after all data for   If the data entered was
)                                               Causes system to accept  the displayed screen has      correct, the system will
                                                the data that has been   been entered.                 process the data entered
.g57j1                                          entered on the screen.                                 and respond with an
.m0L99v4c2                                                                                             Advisory message or, if
----------------------------------------------------------                                             the data entered requests
.v8                                                                                                    the next lower level
.m11L77                                                                                                screen, that screen will
.o10                                                                                                   be displayed.
PURPOSE:  To provide an operator with a means of performing                                            If the data entered was
specific functions by pressing a single key.                                                          incorrect, the system will
                                                                                                      respond with an error
.m0L99v4c2i0b3                                                                                          message.
----------------------------------------------------------
.v8                                        2    Function key F3.         Press F3 when help is re-     There are 7 HELP screens
                                                Requests HELP infor-     quired.                       available. Each time F3
.m0L20c2                                         mation. This is only                                  is pressed the next HELP
Item                                            available for the "Display                             screen will be displayed.
No.                                             Data" screen.
.c                                         3    Function key SF5 (Shifted  Press and hold the shift     The currently displayed
1                                               F5). Allows the operator  key, press F5.                screen will be printed.
.L22                                            to request a printed copy
.m18b4c2                                         of the currently displayed
Field                                           screen.
Description
                                           4    Function key F15.        Press F15                     Redisplays current screen
Function key F1.                                Redisplays the current                                 and discards any pre-
Causes system to accept the data that has been entered on the   screen, allowing the                   viously entered data.
screen.                                         operator to re-enter data.
.m44b7c2
Operator                                    5    Function key F16.       Press F16                     Displays a new screen and
Action                                          Displays a data entry                                  discards any data entered
                                                screen one level higher.                               on old screen.
Press F1 after all data for the displayed screen has been

              1                            ACME Computer Manual          4-1                08/20/84
```

*Columnar input with text can be accomplished with program MagicBind and a
daisy wheel printer. Control codes placed before each portion of text tell the
printer how that text should be formatted and the column in which it should
appear in the final copy.*

COMPANIES AND PROGRAMS

☐ **SWEET-P PLOTTER**

Enter Computers, Inc.
6867 Nancy Ridge Dr.
San Diego, CA 92121
(619) 450-0601

☐ **SOFTWARE MODIFICATIONS**

C.I. Software
1380 Garnet Ave. #E149
San Diego, CA 92109
(619) 483-6384

☐ **PRINTERS**

C.Itoh Electronics, Inc.
5301 Beethoven St.
Los Angeles, CA 90066
(213) 306-6700

☐ **Digital Research, Inc.**

160 Central Ave.
Pacific Grove, CA 93950
(408) 649-5500

For Daisy Wheel and Thimble
Letter Quality Printers

☐ **MAGICPRINT and MAGICBIND**

Computer EdiType Systems
509 Cathedral Parkway
New York, NY 10025
Distributed by Lifeboat Assoc.
1651 Third Ave.
New York, NY 10022

15. Utilities and Working Hints

A computer is supposed to make everything soooo simple. No more misfiled folders, no more file cabinets to flail through, no lost information. Everything instantly available with the punch of a key. True?

Well. Not quite. You probably discovered holes in that theory early in the game. Maybe it's gotten easier, but not necessarily simpler.

That dumb pile of hardware that's supposed to be so darned intelligent, why does it lose files, forget which disk has which file, get glitches you can't conquer? Lucky it's desk height or it would be full of kick marks.

No matter how smart it's *supposed* to be, it still needs you to tell it what to do. It can store millions of characters, and scores of documents on a disk, but locating them again often seems like a job for Scotland Yard. Is there a way to put things someplace and find them again? Is there a way to overcome the new set of frustrations that a computer brings into every user's life.

There can be. It takes systems. And organization.

And utilities.

Yep. That's what the programs are called that help you "keep house" and make life with a word processor more workable. You're already familiar with utilities included with your disk operating system: directory, erase, rename, save, type, status or check, copy, compare, format, etc. But there are many more that will make the relationship more successful.

After the first few months with a word processor most people discover that floppy disks fill up with files quickly and disks pile up. Considering that each file is given a cryptic name it is easy to forget what's in each file. Soon you wonder which letters mean what, where a certain file is, which went to whom, what went with what.

If only . . . you could tag a file with a caption. If only you could catalog the disks. If only it were easier to move files from one disk to another and be sure of what you were doing. If only you could rename a file as you go through a list instead of one by one. The "if only's" could fill a disk of their own.

Fortunately, you're not alone. Many people have tackled the "if only" monster and tamed it by providing a variety of "utility" programs that cater to almost everyone's "if only" wishes. And there will be more.

Many of these utilities are available as "public domain" software, available free or for a minimal disk copying charge through a users' group. You can also find them on remote bulletin board services (RBBS) and you can download them to your computer using a modem and compatible communications software. (See Chapter 16.)

Commercial software utilities exist and these are advertised and listed in the magazines dealing with the system you use. Refer to "utility" programs.

Compile a list of your "if only" wishes, then seek the utilities that will accomplish those chores. Following are several popular utility programs; the first group consists of programs that are in the public domain that you can acquire for the asking from a users' group. The programs in the second group are available from software companies and are well worth investigating.

A catalog program will help you keep track of which files are on which disk. Each disk is named with letters or numerals that appear as the first file in the directory. The catalog program reads that name, and places all files in a data base of its own. Request the location of a file by name or part of a file name, with wild card symbols; the program will show you where it is.

After each work session, when files are added or deleted, that disk should be read by the catalog program to keep the catalog updated.

PUBLIC DOMAIN UTILITIES

Master Catalog

MASTCAT stands for "master catalog." You assign a number or letter and number to each disk in a form the catalog program can read. At the end of a work session when new files are added, run MASTCAT with your work disk and all files will be cataloged by file name and disk number.

When you want to find a file, you can request it in many different formats: by file name, disk number, total file. If you don't remember the exact name of a file you can use an * as a "wild card."

For example, to locate all files beginning with "PA" you can request: A> CAT PA*.*

All files beginning with PA on every disk that has been catalogued will appear on your screen.

Directory

D.COM stands for "Directory." This gem of a program is far superior to the DIR. directory program provided with the operating systems. It lists and alphabetizes all files on a disk and provides the number of K bytes in each file. The bottom has a tally of the number of entries and bytes used and the total number of each that remain. It's a combination of a

The DIRectory provided as a utility with the DOS is not nearly as efficient as a directory program that is in the public domain. It may be called D. or DX. with .COM or .EXE or other extension name of your operating system. D.COM in the CP/M system is illustrated in the top of the photo; observe that files are alphabetized with the number of K bytes occupied by each file. Two status lines below give additional information. Compare it with the bottom list, DIR, which is not alphabetized and offers no status information. The same program is offered for MSDOS systems.

```
NSWEEP  -  Version 1.99    10/07/1983
          (c) Dave Rand, 1983
             Edmonton, Alberta
A - Retag files          I Q - Squeeze/Unsqueeze tagged files
B - Back one file        I R - Rename file(s)
C - Copy file            I S - Check remaining space
D - Delete file          I T - Tag file for transfer
E - Erase T/U files      I U - Untag file
F - Find file            I V - View file
L - Log new disk/user    I W - Wildcard tag of files
N - Mass file copy       I Y - Set file status.
P - Print file           I ? - Display this help
X - Exit to CP/M          I cr, sp - Forward one file


    20. A0: PETPEEVE.COL    4K I f  Find what? look*.*

    21. A0: LOOKUP  .COM    4K I
    22. A0: MAILMRGE.OVR   16K I t  Tagged files =    24K (  17K).
    23. A0: MAINDICT.CMP  136K I
    24. A0: MARKFIX .COM    4K I t  Tagged files =    28K (  28K).
    25. A0: NASWPR  .       4K I u  Tagged files =    28K (  28K).
    26. A0: NSWP    .COM    8K I
    27. A0: PATCHWS .       4K I c  Copy to drive/user? _
                                                              0:16:53
```

NSWP, or NEWSWEEP, is a file management program in the public domain. The menu, at the top, indicates the various procedures it can accomplish. Each file is presented as you hit the spacebar or the <CR> and you place the letter for the command next to the file.

directory and status of the disk. Place a copy of D.COM on every disk and you won't be able to get along without it.

Newsweep

NSWP.COM is a version of an earlier public domain program called SWEEP, both written by Dave Rand of Edmonton, Alberta, Canada. In day-to-day use, it negates the need for the comparable disk operating system utilities and performs them all much more graciously. Consider that if you wished to perform several different tasks on the files on one disk, such as rename, copy, erase, you would have to input several different commands and deal with each file individually, or with those sharing some naming in common.

With NEWSWEEP, the directory appears, one file after another as you hit the return key, and you can request any operation on any file, one after another. You can also tag several files and then deal with them as a group using a multiple command. You can move the files to different user areas, change the logged disks, and squeeze and unsqueeze a file (to make more room on a disk).

Unerase

If you have ever accidentally erased a disk, UNERASE will be able to recover it and replace it on the disk and in your directory *provided* you haven't written another file over it or turned off your machine. It is the answer to "Ooops! What did I do?" Similar programs are titled Recover, Undelete, etc.

Findbad

Sometimes a sector on a disk will become damaged in some unexplainable, mysterious way and your system will give you a message "BDOS ERROR, bad sector on B" or similar ghastly wording. It can be impossible to get past that sector. If that disk is filled with vital information, it's pull-out-hair time. You won't go bald as quickly if you keep a copy of FINDBAD on a work disk. Invoke the command FINDBAD with the disk letter and it will read the bad disk and lock out the offensive sector. Next time, the disk drive will bypass that sector. You'll lose access to the information written on the sector, but that's only a few characters. Usually you can recoup those from your own memory or your own logic. Generally, you don't lose the entire disk and all files. There are exceptions, but it's a better utility than none at all.

These are only a smattering of the many utilities available in the public domain. You may find others. Life can be made much simpler when disks are organized.

INDUSTRY UTILITIES PROGRAMS

All of the above have their counterparts in programs that are offered for sale. It is a sad fact that some programmers begin with the public domain utilities, add a few nuances and routines, copyright the programs, and distribute them as original software. About all they do that public domain software doesn't do is separate the consumer from his money.

However, many excellent programmers write utility programs that are well worth the investment. Evaluate them by the ads, by reviews in magazines. Compare notes with other users to learn:

What programs do they use most often?
What do they like most about the program?
What is it used for?
What does it purport to do that it doesn't?
How efficient is it?
How much disk space does it require?
How is the documentation?
Will it really accomplish what I want or is this wishful thinking?

NORTON UTILITIES for the IBM PC include assorted capabilities all on one disk. There are programs that will unerase, fix a disk, search and repair, display the file, rename, mark time, sort, and more. From Peter W. Norton, 2210 Wilshire Blvd., Santa Monica, CA 90403. $80

MORE SHORTCUTS

Here are ideas to make living with a computer more efficient.

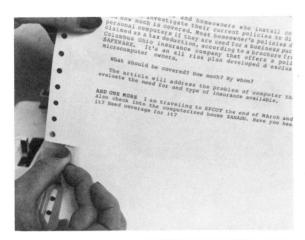

Separate continuous form paper at the serration by flicking the edge with your thumb and forefinger.

Tear edges clean from continuous form paper by bending the serrated portion over the square edge of a desk and then pull down on the punched edge.

To use the second side of a single-sided disk, use a paper punch to make a hole on the opposite side of the jacket on an 8-inch disk. Make the hole for a 5¼-inch disk and clip a notch at the opposite side of the existing notch.

16. Typesetting from Word Processing

The process of setting type for printing has undergone many changes since Gutenberg developed his movable type printing press back in the fifteenth century. The billions of leaded fonts that were laboriously placed into wooden frames by generations of typesetters have been replaced by high technology. Fonts and frames are now antique collectors' items.

The procedure for setting type directly via computers is well established in industries that use high-volume printing: newspaper, magazine, and legal publishing. Often, the procedure is so computerized the copy may never appear as ink image on paper until the finished pages roll off the presses.

A tour of a large newspaper office and its printing facilities will prove worthwhile for an overall understanding of electronic publishing if it can be arranged. The equipment is large, with terminals that display a two-page spread of the newspaper on one screen. The designer requests copy written for an issue and it appears on his terminal. He can manipulate the copy on screen to allow space for illustrations, change the type in one section, rearrange columns, change column size, alter the typeface of titles, and much more. It's all accomplished with the cursor and keyboard.

Think about the time and manpower hours of tedious, repetitive work required using old methods. Take only one of the above tasks. What happens when there is a column of copy that is too long for one page? The makeup editor would have to cut and paste galleys, or edit copy to fit the space. After physically establishing the layout from galleys, the type would be reset. A new set of proofs might be required before the copy was finally "put to bed" and sent to the printer.

With computer systems, once the copy is in the computer's memory, the designer can juggle the copy in infinite ways so he knows exactly how the finished page will appear before it is typeset. There is time to change formats should newsbreaks occur that require last-minute editing.

Computers that can manipulate full pages of text for newspaper, magazine, and book page layouts are still in the domain of the large company. Bringing the capabilities of big systems to the micro and mini markets are the target of programmers and equipment manufacturers. The technology is filtering down to price ranges that are practical for smaller businesses.

"CONVERSION" TYPESETTING

Computerized typesetting from a word processor is called "conversion" typesetting. It reduces costs by reducing labor and time required. When a disk is properly prepared, no human intervention is needed to change typed copy to printed word. The entire operation takes a fraction of the time it would require for a compositor to work from a paper manuscript and correct it. Rekeyboarding and proofreading are eliminated because the copy on disk is accurately matched, character for character, by the typesetting operation.

The written document is prepared with a word processor and saved on a disk. Special "translation" codes are placed in that document on disk to instruct the typesetting machine.

These codes indicate, to the typesetting machine, the size and style of print to use, where to place titles, when to indent, when to begin a new chapter, and so forth. The codes are, to the electronic medium, similar to symbols a page designer would use on hard copy with an editing marker.

Translation codes can vary by a specific typesetter's requirements. Generally they would look something like this: The code %CN would tell the typesetter to begin a new chapter. <CFTRI> would ask that the font be changed to Times Roman italics <EP> would mean end paragraph/ paragraph indent.

Some systems can also address line art and pictures in addition to text. These require different print technologies that interact with the automatic typesetting. If you delve further into electronic typesetting you will discover services such as laser platemaking that can create logos and illustrations that may be coupled with the text type setting.

WHAT IS THE WRITER'S RESPONSIBILITY?

The writer-editor-designer-typesetter route is being used more often in all publishing businesses that produce specialized magazines, books, newsletters, manuals, etc. The writer located in one place sends the copy to a recipient anywhere in the country by either of two procedures.

1. He can send copy using telecommunications services directly from his modem and computer to a publisher or a printer who has the equipment to accept it.

2. He can send the floppy disk, with the copy on it, to the publisher or printer. If the printer has a compatible system there is no problem. If not, the disk has to be converted to one that the host operating system can read.

This all sounds marvelous. And it is when all people and systems involved know the rules and interface procedures. But it is not without problems.

People who use word processors are not usually versed in coding a document for the printer. They do not have the training for, or wish to worry about, the page layout. That's up to the publisher and page designer. Therefore, many publishing offices maintain personnel trained to convert the writer's on-disk document using the codes required for a specific printer output.

However, many companies that buy large-volume printing—publishers, advertising agencies, public relations firms, convention planners, and similar companies—can work directly with printers. When the word processing operator learns to code a manuscript it will save the company money. It is comparable to learning the commands in a host word processing program.

QUESTIONS AND ANSWERS ABOUT TELETYPESETTING

There are some industry standards for printing from computerized files. A summary of questions and answers about electronic printing will help clarify what may be involved.

☐ What is Teletypesetting?

Teletypesetting is designed to receive a typeset manuscript, without rekeying, from remote terminals in a time and cost effective manner. The manuscript must have codes; the typesetter must have a table that will read these codes so that it knows what is wanted. It must have instructions about the size of the page, the size of type, the length of a line, the number of lines on a page, where titles and subtitles are to be placed, indents marked, chapters begun, etc.

The procedure is referred to by many names—electronic typesetting, electronic publishing, computer typesetting, etc.

☐ **What are the advantages of this service?**

Quality, turnaround time, minimum investment, and price. All jobs are produced on computerized phototypesetters. When manuscripts are prepared to specifications, and require no manual intervention by typesetters, they can usually be produced the day they are received. Costs can be reduced by 50 percent or more.

☐ **Can typeset business forms, ads, and small custom printing jobs be typeset in this manner?**

Most systems are capable of producing virtually any kind of work that a client might require. The question is whether the client's operators have the experience and skill necessary to provide the complex typographic coding necessary for such work in a cost effective manner and, secondly, whether the time spent developing the formulas required is economically justifiable. In most cases, it may be as cost effective to typeset "from scratch" special forms using traditional typographic procedures.

☐ **Is there any restriction as to the size job that should be done by this method?**

The main consideration is cost effectiveness. Most printing companies have a minimum make-ready charge for each order received, but many jobs may be included on a single transmission which spreads the impact of this charge.

☐ **How does the system operate?**

The printing company will have a private, or national, telecommunications network. Each client is assigned a user name and password which allows him to access the network. He may then produce manuscripts on a remote terminal, edit them to his satisfaction, and send them over the network to an electronic post office box, which is a central computer storage bank. The publisher retrieves the manuscripts from the storage banks into its phototypesetting system for code translation and typesetting.

☐ **What kind of remote terminals can be used?**

Virtually any word processor or personal computer equipped with communications capabilities (modem and software) can transmit manuscripts directly to a publisher, or to an intermediate electronic service that can convert the file to another system.

☐ **How soon can you send copy?**

After the user has a name and password, translation tables for the user's specific terminal must be established. These are needed so the printer can receive a sample document with the characters coded. Test transmissions must be sent to be sure all is working properly. That may take a couple of weeks depending on the printing company, its methods, and your ability to set up the information and communications system required.

☐ Can manuscripts be sent as they appear in the word processor?

This depends on the degree of cost savings you want to achieve and the typographic control you want to retain. Manuscripts can be received in three ways:

1. Without any intervention by the printer.
2. Partial intervention by the printer.
3. Total intervention by the printer.

It is logical that the less manual intervention by the printer, the lower the cost.

The choice depends on the experience and skill of the person who prepares the document and on the complexity of the manuscript. It's good practice to submit hard copy as well as disk so that if there are questions by the printer, necessary coding changes can be added before the copy is printed. This is especially true in complex manuscripts, such as instruction manuals, text with formulas, and any that require careful style and layout attention.

☐ How does one know what fonts, formats, and print output are available?

The printing company provides the client with a booklet showing sample formats, each with a format number. The user selects the format number and that number dictates the appearance of the published item. Additional codes can be inserted to override some of the basic default codes. Many of the procedures, such as hyphenation and page numbering, are accomplished automatically by the system without coding.

☐ Will the client see proofs?

Absolutely. Proofs may be sent directly to a client by overnight courier. Some printers have cooperating offices in major cities. The proofs are sent to these offices where the client can pick them up. Corrections can be marked on the galleys, or if they are minimal and speed is important, they can be called in to the main plant.

☐ Where does one find these services?

Companies that offer conversion typesetting may be found in the classified pages of telephone books in major cities. National companies will generally advertise in magazines and newspapers that circulate to the print buying and publishing businesses. Because copy can be sent electronically, working with companies at a distance from the home office is no problem.

The services offered and the cost and time-saving implications in the area of computerized publishing are vast. Anyone who is considering self-publishing or who buys printing would be remiss if the potential of these services were not investigated.

17. Ergonomics — Health, Stress, and Other Factors

s growing numbers of businesses, from airline companies to zoos, input and output information via terminals and telecommunications, many physical and psychosomatic complaints have emerged among employees. In the past few years a new body of statistics, terms, and forecasts has surfaced citing the effect of the computer on users' health. Ergonomics, a science that deals with adapting work conditions to suit the worker, has addressed the computer and its work place. What far-reaching effects do ergonomics considerations have on the design of our offices, rooms, lighting, and furniture? How does it affect the word processing environment? Who is responsible for the health of the individual in an office? Is it time for managers, designers, insurance companies, to become alert to the health hazards of computers? Is it time for those of us who work with computers to evaluate our own surroundings and work habits?

The original trickle of literature that dealt with the subject has become a torrent of information with a resounding warning that *everyone* should be concerned with computeritis and other terminal ailments. Phobias, stress, depression are chronicled by psychiatrists and psychologists who pursue changing mental attitudes. Eyes, teeth, ears, necks, backs, legs, and general circulation are affected directly. And there are marital problems, too, What are they? How should they be handled?

MENTAL STRESS

Fears and stresses are vocalized by patients and reported by psychologists who see these problems emerging. The terms "computerphobia" and "cyberphobia" are used to describe a range of fears.

It begins when people first consider adding a computer to their lives. Do they need one? If the decision is affirmative, shopping for computers can reduce the strongest person to a bundle of nerves and stress. Nothing in our past experience has prepared us for the decisions to be made. The procedures are fraught with uncertainty, the necessity to cram new information into a short learning span, the expense involved, and a host of associated factors.

Those who study the effects of high technology in society report that age and position are intricately woven into stress patterns. Executives tolerate computers brought into a business for data processing, word processing, and networking, where they are used by specific personnel. But for many executives, especially those over the age of fifty, it is anathema to think about learning to use the machine to write their own letters or reports, to develop their own sales charts and graphs. They are used to pushing a button and asking someone else to do it or asking them to bring them what they need.

User's fears of computer infiltration are compounded by more fears; perhaps if they don't accept them, they will be displaced by someone younger.

To counteract these real fears many companies send their executives to special training seminars away from the office. Why not in the office? A vice-president at a Dallas bank says, "We find it easier to cure computerphobia among our executives if we train them at centers away from the office. To have our executives fumble over keyboard input, become frustrated with program directives, to ask subordinates for help, is demeaning. We have to provide a private place for them to conquer their fears, overcome their timidity, and learn to communicate in the computerized office."

Another source of stress is the frequent breakdown of some types of equipment. Most employees do not regard these "down times" as unexpected vacations. Instead they worry that the frequent malfunctions will prevent them from completing their work and that they will be blamed.

There's no one cure-all, but there are precautions management can take. Companies should be aware of potential problems, recognize them as they begin to occur and guide the person to the right kind of help. Large companies should retain industrial psychologists for their employees and see that they are used.

PHYSICAL PROBLEMS

Studies of physical ailments already attributed to the computer are appearing in medical and dental journals with increasing frequency.

The effect of terminals has come under serious scrutiny. A compilation of articles appeared in the publication *Current Controversy* titled

"Are Video Display Terminals *Safe?*" The consensus is that the terminals themselves are safe, it's how people use them that must be carefully monitored.

Another by the American Council on Science and Health titled "Health and Safety Aspects of Video Display Terminals" addresses problems with straightforward answers.

There have been adverse publicity and claims in Canadian newspapers about the effect of a pregnant woman's exposure to VDTs on an unborn fetus. But Dr. Ernest G. Letourneau, writing in the Canadian Medical Association *Journal,* believes these claims are unsupported and have led to much unnecessary concern, particularly among women. "VDTs emit no ionizing radiation [X-rays]. There is no evidence that at the detected levels the nonionizing radiation emitted from VDTs can produce biological effects or pose any hazard to health. Thus, in the absence of a cause it is hard to establish a link between VDTs and cataracts or birth defects. . . . They are no more dangerous than the monochrome TV sets found in homes and they carry no radiation hazard."

Eyestrain

A study sponsored by Verbatim Corporation, a supplier of magnetic data storage media, was conducted by Group Attitudes Corporation. In a sample of 1,263 office workers in large, medium, and small companies throughout the country, the main concern was eyestrain (63.4 percent of the respondents) and backstrain (36.3 percent). Nearly 8 in 10 respondents (70.1 percent) called for better lighting for those working with automated machines and 78.8 percent favored periodic rest breaks.

Many also commented that management seldom consulted office staff on the design of work space or structuring the work day to improve working conditions and minimize stress.

The U.S. Department of Health and Human Services report, along with other recent studies, substantiates Verbatim's findings and points to "debilitating visual fatigue as the number one computer related health problem in the country." The problem is so widespread that several states are currently considering legislation to control ergonomics conditions; they are recommending vision screening requirements to protect office workers, according to the Titmus Optical Company of Petersburg, Virginia. Vision screening recommendations include free initial examinations for all full-time VDT operators, with annual checkups mandatory. Prescription glasses would be supplied by the employer.

Most terminals are operated in less than ideal conditions that include glare and reflections on the screen. Sometimes a person becomes so involved with the word and number play he doesn't realize that an overhead light fixture, a sunlight-flooded window, perhaps a white shirt, are being reflected in the screen.

"Computer-related eye problems are under scrutiny as an area for new questioning and treatment," emphasizes Dr. Aaron Steinberg, an optometrist in Vista, California, who has researched the subject. He points out that the CRT's light letters on a black or green background require constant eye adjustment as the jump is made from the screen to the usual printed black letters on white.

The U.S. government survey notes eye movement from copy to keyboard to screen requires that the eye refocus or "accommodate" to changes in distance, color, brightness, and character size as many as 33,000 times in an average work day. According to some experts, visual display terminals create higher visual demands than any other previous working tool. It becomes most serious with employees past the age of thirty-four.

What can you do about it? Essentially, try to reduce or eliminate glare. Dr. Steinberg recommends that computer operators wear glasses with tinted lenses or those that continually adjust to changing light reflections. A light pink tint on lenses will also help. For people who wear bifocals, the problems can be compounded with some complaints of double vision. See your optometrist and tell him you work with a computer. Let him diagnose your special needs.

Look *into* the blank screen; *not at it.* Look for reflections and other light distortions. Do you see overhead lights? windows? shirts? belt buckles? If so, try to eliminate them. Change the position of the terminal in relation to the lights. Hang shades over windows that might be directly behind the terminal so they can be pulled down sufficiently to kill the glare. Keep a black apron or poncho type pullover available if clothes reflect in the screen. You may be able to purchase a non-glare screen for the terminal.

During the day, readjust the screen's contrast for brightness as the light changes and also to give your eyes a change. When screens become dusty and fingerprinted, clean them.

Try to limit the time you spend in front of the terminal without a break. If you work for someone, ten-minute breaks are a built-in aid. When you work for yourself it is possible to sit in front of the screen for three to four hours without moving. Watch for eye twitching at the end of a day; if it appears, get adequate rest and don't spend the evening watching television. Take more frequent breaks from the terminals. In addition, use adjustable tables and chairs, temperature, and noise controls to help reduce overall stress situations.

Backache, Neck Ache, Lower Leg Numbness

Backaches, neck aches, and lower leg problems are not only computer specific, but they can be exacerbated by sitting at the terminal for long hours. Executives who normally were not chair-bound in precomputer days register frequent complaints, not realizing the possible source of the problem.

The Sakata color monitor tilts up and down, swivels right and left and to 90 degrees. It can be placed on a monitor stand to raise it higher than the desktop.
Courtesy of Sakata USA Corp.

Sitting in one position too long will result in aches and pains up and down the 24 movable bones in your spine that extend from the top of your neck to the bottom of your back. Each bone has hundreds of muscles and nerves extending from it so that your shoulders can ache, too.

Reevaluate the terminal's placement. If the screen is too high, an awkward head position can produce tension and strain along your shoulders and in your neck. Place your screen so it is straight ahead of you or slightly lower than your head so you are looking down at it in a more comfortable position for your neck.

Become acutely aware of your chair. Is it a comfortable height? Does it give your spine adequate support? Is it on wheels and does the seat swivel so you can easily move from one unit to another rather than contort your body to twist from the terminal to your desk?

Change your position frequently. Get up and walk around. Stretch. Do knee bends, push yourself off a wall with your feet placed about 20 inches away from the wall, heels flat on the floor to stretch the leg and hamstring muscles.

Bruxism

Bruxism is the technical name for "grinding teeth." Its cause? Tension. Bruxism symptoms may be aching teeth anywhere in the mouth depending upon your individual bite pattern. It can affect the ears. too. Patients who are "bruxists" complain of shooting pains in their jaws and into their ears. The symptoms may not occur while you are at the machine; they often show up when you are relaxing or even when you try to sleep.

See your dentist if you have a touch of these symptoms. He may fit you with a "bite plate," a small, readily removable plastic piece that conforms to the roof of your mouth and does not show at all. You wear it while you work or sleep, and remove it when you eat. It keeps your teeth from coming together so you can't grind them. If your dentist doesn't think of a bite plate, ask him. It's a simple solution for preventing what could be a complicated problem.

COMPUTERS AND MARRIAGE PROBLEMS

When a branch of the U.S. Navy in San Diego installed new computer graphics equipment in one of the offices, programmers were so fascinated with the equipment they stayed beyond their normal work hours. When wives complained, management had to shut the offices at 7 P.M. so the programmers would leave. A potential crisis was averted.

Jokes and cartoons about people being "married to a computer" are already clichés. A woman can be as guilty as a man, though men outnumber women. When a spouse is replaced by a disk and chips, trouble is in the air, report psychiatrists and attorneys who have already handled many such cases. How to cope? Recognize the symptoms. If your spouse is complaining about the many hours you sit glued to a terminal, there may be cause for concern. For the sake of sanity, place a limit on the time you give to the computer in relation to your spouse. Or, buy another terminal and use them together. Find programs that will interest the other person, and take the time to teach him or her how to use them.

If any of the above are evident in your relationships or among conditions where you work, it is important to perform serious troubleshooting by questioning individuals and discussing the problem with management. Once diagnosed, computeritis and other terminal ailments can be dealt with in a positive manner so they become harmless to everyone's health and happiness.

SUMMARY OF WORK PLACE HEALTH CONDITIONS

The National Institute for Occupational Safety and Health (NIOSH) has the following recommendations for video display terminal work places:

Work Station Design
Station should be adaptable to the individual operator.
The chair should have an adjustable seat height, backrest height, and tension.
Keyboard and screen height should be independently adjustable.

The trend to detached keyboards and monitors that tilt and swivel is in response to greater interest in the ergonomics of the work place. The CIT 101e monochrome video display terminal has a 14-inch screen; the unit can be easily positioned with a 10-degree tilt and 60-degree swivel that works fluidly, not in fixed increments.
Courtesy of CIE Terminals

Screen brightness and contrast should be operator controllable. Illumination should be approximately 500–700 lux.

Glare Control

There should be drapes, shades, or blinds over windows.
The terminal should be properly placed with respect to windows and lights.
Antiglare filters may be needed on VDT screens.
Reevaluate and redirect glare from lighting fixtures.

Rest Periods

A 15-minute break should be required after two hours of continuous VDT work under moderate visual demands and or moderate work load.
A 15-minute rest break after one hour of continuous VDT work under high visual demand work loads.

Visual Testing

There should be periodic visual examinations of workers to ascertain and correct any vision changes as a result of working with VDTs.

18. Business Opportunities in Word Processing

lmost any aspect of computers can lead to new business opportunities. Think of how many services exist because of Henry Ford's invention. Computers are believed to be as important a development as the automobile and the basis for thousands of allied businesses and services. They are blossoming already (some have died), but the opportunities are present for a person who has ideas, motivation, and the money that may be required to begin.

KINDS OF BUSINESSES

A study of businesses already offered may inspire you to think of more. Jot down as many potential services as you can think of. Add any that you wish existed for your purposes. Observe ads in computer, business, education, research, and similar magazines. Look under data processing, computers, home computers, and similar listings in the telephone books of major cities. Attend computer conventions to learn what other people are doing, how they started, how they promote their business. The following ideas may help you discover an area where you have a service to offer.

Word Processing Service

The most obvious area for a business is to offer word processing services for other people. It is akin to a typing service or a typing pool but expanded with word processing. The extent of the service can vary. There are those where you, or someone you employ, does the actual typing. There are services that rent time on a word processor so someone can do his or her own typing. Such a service is usually used by writers, short-term users of word processing, or companies that have a work overload for their own equipment.

"Special" typing services are in demand and may require you to know how to use software that someone else may not have. An example? Script writing is a specialized aspect of word processing and there are specific programs that will format text exactly as required, such as Scriptor and Scriptwriter. Programs such as MagicBind and MagicPrint, already mentioned, or a word processing program with preset style formats may be enough to help you launch a business supplying carefully formatted documents to clients.

Form letter mailings for businesses can be an opportunity. Attorneys, physicians, debt collectors, city agencies, churches, civic organizations; anyone who has neither the staff nor the equipment to accomplish mass mailings would be a client for a word processing business. Their mailing lists could be maintained, too.

People who can key typesetting commands into finished documents on disk are already in demand by printing companies. Special programs help accomplish this task.

Teaching—Training

For anyone familiar with one or more word processing systems, there's good money to be made in teaching what you know to others. Teaching and training (see Chapter 13) is an ongoing need in many business offices. Some use outside teachers and bring them in as new employees need training. Teachers may be paid on an hourly basis or as a consultant with an annual salary who can be called upon as needed.

Word processing teachers are needed by companies that teach their own system to new buyers, by adult education schools, and by computer schools. Temporary employment agencies are also a source for teachers; agencies train their temporary help in a variety of word processing programs so they have people they can send to meet the need of specific equipment among their clients. Computer dealers require teachers to train personnel in companies that purchase their systems.

Job Placement Agency

You may be in a position to open a job placement agency or a temporary employment agency which will supply word processing operators to different companies for permanent or part-time employment.

Seminars

Learning how to use many of the programs mentioned in this book will expand your word processing expertise. Knowing which programs will help other people, and explaining how they might help productivity, could be a subject for office management seminars. Continue to investigate as many programs as you can and add these to the information you offer.

Consulting

Consulting about different word processing programs in various environments has proven a smart business for many people. You will have to know many programs well and which do what. Consulting requires evaluating requirements for a company or an individual, then advising them as to the best software for their needs. A consultant may also assist clients in hardware to buy before programs are purchased. An overall knowledge of computers, programs, printers, and other peripherals is required.

Supplies

For those with ample contacts, marketing word processing supplies to other companies is becoming big business. People who are in it had to begin somewhere. Established stationery suppliers had only to add computer supplies to their marketing. But there is always room for suppliers of paper, ribbons, furniture. There's a business to be offered in designing stationery and applying it to computer stock.

Ribbon Reinking

There are several reinking devices on the market for printer ribbons. A ribbon reinking service could save money for many companies who may not realize that ribbon cartridges can be recycled. (See Chapter 10.)

Work Station Designing

Chapter 17, about ergonomics, emphasizes the importance of proper work station design; desks the proper height and depth for a computer and keyboard, and proper lighting. But there's even more to consider in a work station. There are electrical loads, static problems, power lines that must be taken across rooms so that people won't trip on them. Some units require turntables to be shared by two or more operators.

Designing work stations for maximum efficiency is one potential business. Couple it with supplies and you're on your way to offering services people want and need.

Programming

Certainly all the desires of word processing operators have not been met. Is there some task you wish could be accomplished but haven't been able to find a program to accomplish it? If your talents are in programming, there may be innovative software you could design that would improve, and work with, software that already exists.

Writing About Word Processing

Editors of word processing publications, computer magazines, newsletters for home, office, education, or covering any specific machine or word processing program, will often carry articles about various aspects of word processing. Study the publications, consult the *Writer's Market* at your library, to learn which magazines seek submissions. Send a letter to one or more publications outlining your ideas and showing the editor you know how to write in their style, which you should determine by studying the magazine. When someone is interested, you're on your way to being a writer.

Documentation Evaluation—Development

Anyone who has struggled through the learning process of several programs quickly appreciates what is good and what is not so good in a manual. Companies who produce manuals often are too close to their subject and seek outside people who will test it and evaluate documentation against a program. Yes, even this is a business. Often, if a person has a writing knack and understands how programs work, he or she can write documentation, too.

Research Service

Not everyone has the time or inclination to learn how to use data banks efficiently to gather the information needed. If they only need research occasionally, they may look for someone who will do it for them. That could be you. Subscribe to one or two popular or specialized services. How do you let potential clients know you can do the research for them? Post notices at a local university library, a medical library, a legal library, an engineering library, among architects. Place notices in newsletters that reach people who may need research services.

EVALUATING A MARKET

Before any sizable business is ventured, a careful study should be made of the market and your ability to sell your service. It's possible that some services, such as teaching at a local school, may not require an actual commitment as a business. However, for any endeavor, the following questions should be addressed.

What do you need to get started?

Can you evaluate the level of business you can handle?

Can you clearly identify a local and/or national market?

Do you have the necessary equipment?

How much can you produce alone?

How will you make your service known?

What is the competition?

What can you charge?

Estimate the hourly time required to complete a project including proof-reading. Figure in overhead.

How will you advertise?

How much volume must you have to make a profit?

What will expenses be?

How will you cope with downtime? Will you have backup equipment available?

Can you get help if you need it?

Will you be able to rent your equipment to others? What will you have to charge in your office?

Will you offer document storage? For how long? For how much?

Will you offer your service from your home as a cottage industry?

Can you share office space or afford a solo office?

How much time? energy? money? do you have?

Word processing is new. Yes. But it's been around long enough to result in a market, in experts, in people who need services. There's every indication that we are only at the threshold of what is going to happen.

Word processing has expanded—there is no size limitation in sight!

List of Trademarks

Apple®
Apricot Computer ACT
ATI Training Power™

Bank Street Writer™
The Benchmark®
BIBLIOGRAPHY™
Blue

CalcStar®
Canon color ink jet
CDEX™
Chameleon
C.I. Software
CIT 80
Computer EdiType
    Systems
CP/M®

Datapro Research Corp.
dBase II® d Base III®
Dest Workless™ Station
Digital Research, Inc.™
DocuMate/Plus™
DocuMentor™
Durango dot matrix™

Easy Writer II™
Easytext
Electric Webster™
Electric Pencil™
ExecuVision®

FancyFont™
The FinalWord
First Draft®
Flip Track®
FOOTNOTE™

Grammatik™

Hewlett-Packard the
    PORTABLE
HexPrintR™

IBM®
IBM PC®
ITT XTRA

Kaypro II™
Key-Fixer™
Key Tronic™
K-Key®

Leading Edge®
Lotus 1-2-3™

MacInker
Macintosh™
MagiCalc™
MagicBind™
MagicIndex™
MailMerge®
Many Key
MasterCalc
MegaWriter™
MicroMailer™
MicroPro Training
    Guides®
Microsoft™
MicroSpell™
Mince™
Monroe System 2000
MONTOP®
MS™DOS
Multicalc

MultiMate™

NCR™ Personal
    Computer
NewsNet®
Norton Utilities™

OMNI-READER™
Open Access™

Palantir™
PC DOS
PC Talk
PeachText™
People Sorter
Perfect Calc™
Perfect File™
Perfect Software™
Perfect Speller™
Perfect Writer™
Plexiglas
P/Mate™
POPPY™
PowerText®
ProKey™
ProofReader™
ProTem Software, Inc.™
"Punctuation" + Style™

Qume®

Radio Shack®
Random House®
    Electronic Thesaurus
Random House
    ProofReader™
Rolodex™
RoseSoft™

Samna Word II

Scriptomatic®

Scriptor

Scriptwriter

The Select™ Processor

Set-FX™

SmartCom II™

SMARTKEY™

SoftStyle

Sorcim®

Spellbinder™

SpellStar®

Spinwriter®

Sprint®

SuperCalc 2™

SuperWriter™

Symphony™

Synonym Finder

Telenet

TeleStar™

TeleVideo™

THE WORD™ Plus

T/Maker™

TRS-80®

TURBODOS

Turbofont

Tymnet

VisiCalc®

Volkswriter®

Word®

Word Index™

Wordnet

WordPerfect

Word Plus-PC™

Word Proof

Word Right

WordStar®

Write-On!

Zobex™

Index